OPPOSING VIEWPOINTS® SERIES

Birth Defects

Other Books of Related Interest:

Opposing Viewpoints Series

At Issue Series

Current Controversies Series

"Congress shall make no law . . . abridging the freedom of speech, or of the press."

First Amendment to the US Constitution

The basic foundation of our democracy is the First Amendment guarantee of freedom of expression. The Opposing Viewpoints Series is dedicated to the concept of this basic freedom and the idea that it is more important to practice it than to enshrine it.

OPPOSING VIEWPOINTS® SERIES

Birth Defects

Noël Merino, Book Editor

GREENHAVEN PRESS
A part of Gale, Cengage Learning

GALE
CENGAGE Learning·

Farmington Hills, Mich • San Francisco • New York • Waterville, Maine
Meriden, Conn • Mason, Ohio • Chicago

GALE
CENGAGE Learning®

Elizabeth Des Chenes, *Director, Content Strategy*
Douglas Dentino, Manager, *New Product*

© 2014 Greenhaven Press, a part of Gale, Cengage Learning.

WCN: 01-100-101

Gale and Greenhaven Press are registered trademarks used herein under license.

For more information, contact:
Greenhaven Press
27500 Drake Rd.
Farmington Hills, MI 48331-3535
Or you can visit our Internet site at gale.cengage.com

For product information and technology assistance, contact us at

Gale Customer Support, 1-800-877-4253
For permission to use material from this text or product, submit all requests online at www.cengage.com/permissions

Further permissions questions can be emailed to permissionrequest@cengage.com

Articles in Greenhaven Press anthologies are often edited for length to meet page requirements. In addition, original titles of these works are changed to clearly present the main thesis and to explicitly indicate the author's opinion. Every effort is made to ensure that Greenhaven Press accurately reflects the original intent of the authors. Every effort has been made to trace the owners of copyrighted material.

Cover image copyright © sfamphoto/Shutterstock.com.

LIBRARY OF CONGRESS CATALOGING-IN-PUBLICATION DATA

Birth defects / Noël Merino, book editor.
    p. cm. -- (Opposing viewpoints)
    Summary: "Opposing Viewpoints: Birth Defects: Opposing Viewpoints is the leading source for libraries and classrooms in need of current-issue materials. The viewpoints are selected from a wide range of highly respected sources and publications"-- Provided by publisher.
    Includes bibliographical references and index.
    ISBN 978-0-7377-4504-7 (hardback) -- ISBN 978-0-7377-4505-4 (paperback)
    1. Abnormalities, Human. 2. Fetus--Abnormalities--Etiology. 3. Obstetrics-- Quality control. I. Noël Merino, editor of compilation.
    RG627.5.B57 2014
    618.3'2686--dc23
                                                2013049047

Printed in the United States of America
1 2 3 4 5 6 7 18 17 16 15 14

Contents

Chapter 3: Should Pregnant Women Undergo Screening for Birth Defects?

Chapter 4: How Should Birth Defects Be Addressed?

Why Consider Opposing Viewpoints?

> "The only way in which a human being can make some approach to knowing the whole of a subject is by hearing what can be said about it by persons of every variety of opinion and studying all modes in which it can be looked at by every character of mind. No wise man ever acquired his wisdom in any mode but this."
>
> *John Stuart Mill*

In our media-intensive culture it is not difficult to find differing opinions. Thousands of newspapers and magazines and dozens of radio and television talk shows resound with differing points of view. The difficulty lies in deciding which opinion to agree with and which "experts" seem the most credible. The more inundated we become with differing opinions and claims, the more essential it is to hone critical reading and thinking skills to evaluate these ideas. Opposing Viewpoints books address this problem directly by presenting stimulating debates that can be used to enhance and teach these skills. The varied opinions contained in each book examine many different aspects of a single issue. While examining these conveniently edited opposing views, readers can develop critical thinking skills such as the ability to compare and contrast authors' credibility, facts, argumentation styles, use of persuasive techniques, and other stylistic tools. In short, the Opposing Viewpoints Series is an ideal way to attain the higher-level thinking and reading skills so essential in a culture of diverse and contradictory opinions.

In addition to providing a tool for critical thinking, Opposing Viewpoints books challenge readers to question their own strongly held opinions and assumptions. Most people form their opinions on the basis of upbringing, peer pressure, and personal, cultural, or professional bias. By reading carefully balanced opposing views, readers must directly confront new ideas as well as the opinions of those with whom they disagree. This is not to argue simplistically that everyone who reads opposing views will—or should—change his or her opinion. Instead, the series enhances readers' understanding of their own views by encouraging confrontation with opposing ideas. Careful examination of others' views can lead to the readers' understanding of the logical inconsistencies in their own opinions, perspective on why they hold an opinion, and the consideration of the possibility that their opinion requires further evaluation.

Evaluating Other Opinions

To ensure that this type of examination occurs, Opposing Viewpoints books present all types of opinions. Prominent spokespeople on different sides of each issue as well as well-known professionals from many disciplines challenge the reader. An additional goal of the series is to provide a forum for other, less known, or even unpopular viewpoints. The opinion of an ordinary person who has had to make the decision to cut off life support from a terminally ill relative, for example, may be just as valuable and provide just as much insight as a medical ethicist's professional opinion. The editors have two additional purposes in including these less known views. One, the editors encourage readers to respect others' opinions—even when not enhanced by professional credibility. It is only by reading or listening to and objectively evaluating others' ideas that one can determine whether they are worthy of consideration. Two, the inclusion of such viewpoints encourages the important critical thinking skill of objectively evaluating an author's credentials and bias. This evaluation will illuminate an author's reasons for taking a particular stance on an issue and will aid in readers' evaluation of the author's ideas.

It is our hope that these books will give readers a deeper understanding of the issues debated and an appreciation of the complexity of even seemingly simple issues when good and honest people disagree. This awareness is particularly important in a democratic society such as ours in which people enter into public debate to determine the common good. Those with whom one disagrees should not be regarded as enemies but rather as people whose views deserve careful examination and may shed light on one's own.

Thomas Jefferson once said that "difference of opinion leads to inquiry, and inquiry to truth." Jefferson, a broadly educated man, argued that "if a nation expects to be ignorant and free . . . it expects what never was and never will be." As individuals and as a nation, it is imperative that we consider the opinions of others and examine them with skill and discernment. The Opposing Viewpoints Series is intended to help readers achieve this goal.

David L. Bender and Bruno Leone,
Founders

Introduction

"Every 4.5 minutes, a baby is born with a birth defect."

—US Centers for
Disease Control and Prevention

Birth defects are congenital malformations, which means that they are present from birth. The malformation may affect the appearance of the physical body or the function of bodily processes, or both. According to the US Centers for Disease Control and Prevention, approximately one in every thirty-three babies born in the United States is born with a birth defect. Birth defects are a leading cause of death in the United States and account for 20 percent of all infant deaths. Not all birth defects are serious, however, and many can be corrected or managed by treatment and/or surgery.

Birth defects can have causes that are genetic, environmental, or both. The exact causes of many birth defects are unknown, although influencing factors have been identified, such as the presence of certain genes and contributing environmental risks to the fetus. Thus, prevention of birth defects can entail genetic screening prior to or after conception, and the adoption of certain health practices by pregnant women and would-be parents. Because of the difficulty of identifying the causes of birth defects—and the likelihood that in many cases there are multiple genetic and environmental causes—prevention of all birth defects is unlikely to be achieved.

One common way of eliminating birth defects, although controversial, is to terminate pregnancies in which a birth defect has been identified. This is a timely issue, discussed at length in the present volume, because of the recent development of noninvasive prenatal genetic tests that can identify certain birth defects as early as nine or ten weeks into a pregnancy. However, the issue of terminating fetuses with birth defects has been around for years, with legal abortion having been in place since the 1973 US Supreme Court case *Roe v. Wade*, and with ultrasound technology and amniocentesis offering information about birth defects, albeit later than is currently available.

The question of what to do when a birth defect is discovered at birth resulted in a major controversy in the 1980s, leading to the passage of legislation that was later ruled unconstitutional by the US Supreme Court. An infant known as Baby Doe was born in Indiana in 1982 with Down syndrome, the effects of which would have required surgery so that the infant could survive. The parents decided to withhold medical treatment, including the surgery, on the advice of their doctor. Other doctors at the hospital, however, disagreed with the decision and the hospital went to court to have medical treatment ordered. The Indiana courts determined that there was no violation of the law and during an appeal of the case, Baby Doe died.

The US surgeon general at the time, C. Everett Koop, spoke out against the withholding of treatment in the Baby Doe case and decided to intervene in a later case in which an infant was born in New York with severe spinal defects in 1983. The parents did eventually allow surgery, and Baby Jane Doe, as she was referred to in the case, survived with severe mental and physical disabilities. The situation resulted in a nationwide controversy over the issue of treatment for newborns with birth defects and the extent to which the government should interfere with the private medical decisions of parents and doctors.

The controversy resulted in passage by the US Congress of the Baby Doe Amendment in 1984, which amended the federal Child Abuse Prevention and Treatment Act to define child abuse as the "withholding of medically indicated treatment from disabled infants with life-threatening conditions." A violation of the Child Abuse Prevention and Treatment Act results in the withholding of federal funds to the state. The US Supreme Court in 1986, however, ruled that the federal government is not allowed "to give unsolicited advice either to parents, to hospitals, or to state officials who are faced with difficult treatment decisions concerning handicapped children," disallowing the kind of intervention taken by Koop with respect to Baby Jane Doe. Nonetheless, the Baby Doe Amendment remains in effect, and most states follow it by having hospital ethics boards involved in cases where there is a withholding of treatment of infants.

The social controversy that resulted from the Baby Doe and Baby Jane Doe cases illustrates the extent of opposing views surrounding the issue of birth defects. Competing ideas on a variety of issues are debated in *Opposing Viewpoints: Birth Defects* in the following chapters: What Are Common Birth Defects?, What Causes Birth Defects?, Should Pregnant Women Undergo Screening for Birth Defects?, and How Should Birth Defects Be Addressed? The views in this anthology offer different perspectives on these issues and illustrate the high level of divergence in American society on this controversial issue.

OPPOSING
VIEWPOINTS®
SERIES

CHAPTER 1

What Are Common Birth Defects?

Chapter Preface

According to the March of Dimes "Global Report on Birth Defects," every year 6 percent of children born worldwide—7.9 million—are born with a serious birth defect of a genetic origin. This number does not include the hundreds of thousands of babies born with birth defects caused after conception, such as from exposure to alcohol or from maternal iodine or folic acid deficiency. The March of Dimes estimates that at least 3.3 million children under the age of five die each year from birth defects and approximately the same number who survive may be disabled for life. However, the incidence of and outcomes for birth defects vary considerably around the world.

More than seven thousand different birth defects of genetic or partially genetic origin have been identified. However, worldwide, five particular birth defects account for one-fourth of all genetic birth defects. The five birth defects, in descending order of incidence worldwide, are: 1) congenital heart defects; 2) neural tube defects (affecting the brain, spine, or spinal cord); 3) the hemoglobin blood disorders, thalassemia and sickle cell disease; 4) Down syndrome; and 5) the human enzyme defect, glucose-6-phosphate dehydrogenase (G6PD) deficiency.

The prevalence of birth defects by country varies widely. According to the March of Dimes report, topping the list with a rate of birth defects of over 75 per 1,000 live births are, in descending order: Sudan, Saudi Arabia, Benin, Burkina Faso, the Occupied Palestinian Territory, United Arab Emirates, Tajikistan, and Iraq. The countries with the lowest rate of birth defects of under 50 per 1,000 live births are, in descending order: Hungary, Israel, the Netherlands, Portugal, the United States, Cuba, New Zealand, Denmark, Slovenia, Norway, Canada, Sweden, the Czech Republic, Belgium, Germany, the United Kingdom, Finland, Spain, Italy, the Russian Federation, Switzerland, Australia, Austria, and France.

The incidence of birth defects, as the above list illustrates, varies drastically between high-income, or industrialized, countries and low- to middle-income, or developing, countries. According to the March of Dimes, low-income countries have approximately 60 percent of the world's total birth defects, middle-income countries have about 34 percent, and birth defects in high-income countries account for only about 6 percent of the world's total birth defects. The outcomes for birth defects are much worse in low- and middle-income countries, where 94 percent of all serious birth defects occur and where 95 percent of the deaths from birth defects occur.

The incidence of and outcomes for birth defects in the United States vary from the global statistics, as the viewpoints in this chapter illustrate. The United States, like other industrialized countries, reported a 46 percent decline in infant mortality rates from 1980 to 2001, similar to other high-income countries; a result of investment in diagnosis, care, and prevention.

| "Congenital heart defects are the most common type of birth defect."

Congenital Heart Defects Are Common Birth Defects

National Heart, Lung, and Blood Institute

In the following viewpoint, the National Heart, Lung, and Blood Institute claims that congenital heart defects are the most common type of birth defect, though most of these defects are simple and require no treatment or are easily fixed. The author gives an overview of the types of congenital heart defects that exist, their causes, their symptoms, and the available treatments. The National Heart, Lung, and Blood Institute, a part of the National Institutes of Health, provides global leadership for a research, training, and education program to promote the prevention and treatment of heart, lung, and blood diseases.

As you read, consider the following questions:

1. According to the National Heart, Lung, and Blood Institute, each year more than how many babies in the United States are born with congenital heart defects?

2. What fraction of babies with Down syndrome have congenital heart defects, according to the author?

"What Are Congenital Heart Defects?," National Heart, Lung, and Blood Institute, National Institutes of Health, July 1, 2011. www.nhlbi.nih.gov.

3. The author gives what four examples of congenital heart defect problems that cardiac surgeons may fix with open-heart surgery?

Congenital heart defects are problems with the heart's structure that are present at birth. These defects can involve:

- The interior walls of the heart

- The valves inside the heart

- The arteries and veins that carry blood to the heart or the body

Congenital Heart Defects

Congenital heart defects change the normal flow of blood through the heart.

There are many types of congenital heart defects. They range from simple defects with no symptoms to complex defects with severe, life-threatening symptoms.

Congenital heart defects are the most common type of birth defect. They affect 8 out of every 1,000 newborns. Each year, more than 35,000 babies in the United States are born with congenital heart defects.

Many of these defects are simple conditions. They need no treatment or are easily fixed. Some babies are born with complex congenital heart defects. These defects require special medical care soon after birth.

The diagnosis and treatment of complex heart defects has greatly improved over the past few decades. As a result, almost all children who have complex heart defects survive to adulthood and can live active, productive lives.

Most people who have complex heart defects continue to need special heart care throughout their lives. They may need to pay special attention to how their condition affects issues such as health insurance, employment, birth control and pregnancy, and other health issues.

In the United States, more than 1 million adults are living with congenital heart defects. . . .

Types of Congenital Heart Defects

With congenital heart defects, some part of the heart doesn't form properly before birth. This changes the normal flow of blood through the heart.

There are many types of congenital heart defects. Some are simple, such as a hole in the septum. The hole allows blood from the left and right sides of the heart to mix. Another example of a simple defect is a narrowed valve that blocks blood flow to the lungs or other parts of the body.

Other heart defects are more complex. They include combinations of simple defects, problems with the location of blood vessels leading to and from the heart, and more serious problems with how the heart develops.

The septum is the wall that separates the chambers on the left and right sides of the heart. The wall prevents blood from mixing between the two sides of the heart. Some babies are born with holes in the septum. These holes allow blood to mix between the two sides of the heart.

Atrial Septal Defect (ASD)

An ASD is a hole in the part of the septum that separates the atria—the upper chambers of the heart. The hole allows oxygen-rich blood from the left atrium to flow into the right atrium, instead of flowing into the left ventricle as it should. Many children who have ASDs have few, if any, symptoms.

ASDs can be small, medium, or large. Small ASDs allow only a little blood to leak from one atrium to the other. They don't affect how the heart works and don't need any special treatment. Many small ASDs close on their own as the heart grows during childhood.

Medium and large ASDs allow more blood to leak from one atrium to the other. They're less likely to close on their own.

About half of all ASDs close on their own over time. Medium and large ASDs that need treatment can be repaired using a catheter procedure or open-heart surgery.

Ventricular Septal Defect (VSD)

A VSD is a hole in the part of the septum that separates the ventricles—the lower chambers of the heart. The hole allows oxygen-rich blood to flow from the left ventricle into the right ventricle, instead of flowing into the aorta and out to the body as it should.

VSDs can be small, medium, or large. Small VSDs don't cause problems and may close on their own. Medium VSDs are less likely to close on their own and may require treatment.

Large VSDs allow a lot of blood to flow from the left ventricle to the right ventricle. As a result, the left side of the heart must work harder than normal. Extra blood flow increases blood pressure in the right side of the heart and the lungs.

The heart's extra workload can cause heart failure and poor growth. If the hole isn't closed, high blood pressure can scar the arteries in the lungs.

Doctors use open-heart surgery to repair VSDs.

Patent Ductus Arteriosus (PDA)

Patent ductus arteriosus (PDA) is a fairly common heart defect that can occur soon after birth. In PDA, abnormal blood flow occurs between the aorta and the pulmonary artery.

Before birth, these arteries are connected by a blood vessel called the ductus arteriosus. This blood vessel is an essential part of fetal blood circulation. Within minutes or up to a few days after birth, the ductus arteriosus closes.

In some babies, however, the ductus arteriosus remains open (patent). The opening allows oxygen-rich blood from the aorta to mix with oxygen-poor blood from the pulmonary artery. This can strain the heart and increase blood pressure in the lung arteries.

A heart murmur might be the only sign of PDA. (A heart murmur is an extra or unusual sound heard during a heartbeat.) Other signs and symptoms can include shortness of breath, poor feeding and growth, tiring easily, and sweating with [little] exertion.

PDA is treated with medicines, catheter-based procedures, and surgery. Small PDAs often close without treatment.

Narrowed Valves

Simple congenital heart defects also can involve the heart's valves. These valves control the flow of blood from the atria to the ventricles and from the ventricles into the two large arteries connected to the heart (the aorta and the pulmonary artery).

Valves can have the following types of defects:

- Stenosis. This defect occurs if the flaps of a valve thicken, stiffen, or fuse together. As a result, the valve cannot fully open. Thus, the heart has to work harder to pump blood through the valve.

- Atresia. This defect occurs if a valve doesn't form correctly and lacks a hole for blood to pass through. Atresia of a valve generally results in more complex congenital heart disease.

- Regurgitation. This defect occurs if a valve doesn't close tightly. As a result, blood leaks back through the valve.

The most common valve defect is pulmonary valve stenosis, which is a narrowing of the pulmonary valve. This valve allows blood to flow from the right ventricle into the pulmonary artery. The blood then travels to the lungs to pick up oxygen.

Pulmonary valve stenosis can range from mild to severe. Most children who have this defect have no signs or symptoms other than a heart murmur. Treatment isn't needed if the stenosis is mild.

In babies who have severe pulmonary valve stenosis, the right ventricle can get very overworked trying to pump blood to the pulmonary artery. These infants may have signs and symptoms such as rapid or heavy breathing, fatigue (tiredness), and poor feeding. Older children who have severe pulmonary valve stenosis may have symptoms such as [unusually fast-occurring] fatigue while exercising.

Some babies may have pulmonary valve stenosis and PDA or ASDs. If this happens, oxygen-poor blood can flow from the right side of the heart to the left side. This can cause cyanosis. Cyanosis is a bluish tint to the skin, lips, and fingernails. It occurs because the oxygen level in the blood leaving the heart is below normal.

Severe pulmonary valve stenosis is treated with a catheter procedure.

Complex Congenital Heart Defects

Complex congenital heart defects need to be repaired with surgery. Advances in treatment now allow doctors to successfully repair even very complex congenital heart defects.

The most common complex heart defect is tetralogy of Fallot, which is a combination of four defects:

- Pulmonary valve stenosis.

- A large VSD.

- An overriding aorta. In this defect, the aorta is located between the left and right ventricles, directly over the

The Genetic Causes of Birth Defects

The heart is one of the first organs to develop in the fetus. At approximately three weeks of gestation, a tiny tube is formed and the fetal heart begins to beat. During the next few days, the tube begins to bend and fold in on itself, forming a loop that roughly takes the shape of the heart. By the 18th week of pregnancy, this tiny tube has molded into all of the basic structures of the heart. It's possible for physicians to detect some heart defects by the 18th week of pregnancy.

Genes contain the sets of instructions that guide the process of development. If these instructions are jumbled, the heart will fail to develop normally. For example, if the instructions for developing the aortic valve are incorrect, the valve may be absent altogether, as in aortic valve atresia, or misshapen, as in aortic valve stenosis.

Scientists are on the verge of discovering the genes that are associated with numerous heart defects. Currently, more than 100 mutations in several genes have been linked with congenital heart defects.

U.S. News & World Report, *February 11, 2009.*

VSD. As a result, oxygen-poor blood from the right ventricle can flow directly into the aorta instead of into the pulmonary artery.

- Right ventricular hypertrophy. In this defect, the muscle of the right ventricle is thicker than usual because it has to work harder than normal.

In tetralogy of Fallot, not enough blood is able to reach the lungs to get oxygen, and oxygen-poor blood flows to the body.

Babies and children who have tetralogy of Fallot have episodes of cyanosis, which can be severe. In the past, when this condition wasn't treated in infancy, older children would get very tired during exercise and might faint. Tetralogy of Fallot is repaired in infancy now to prevent these problems.

Tetralogy of Fallot must be repaired with open-heart surgery, either soon after birth or later in infancy. The timing of the surgery depends on how narrow the pulmonary artery is.

Children who have had this heart defect repaired need lifelong medical care from a specialist to make sure they stay as healthy as possible. . . .

Causes of Congenital Heart Defects

Doctors often don't know why congenital heart defects occur.

Heredity may play a role in some heart defects. For example, a parent who has a congenital heart defect may be more likely than other people to have a child with the defect. Rarely, more than one child in a family is born with a heart defect.

Children who have genetic disorders, such as Down syndrome, often have congenital heart defects. In fact, half of all babies who have Down syndrome have congenital heart defects.

Smoking during pregnancy also has been linked to several congenital heart defects, including septal defects.

The Signs and Symptoms of Defects

Many congenital heart defects cause few or no signs and symptoms. A doctor may not even detect signs of a heart defect during a physical exam.

Some heart defects do cause signs and symptoms. They depend on the number, type, and severity of the defects. Severe defects can cause signs and symptoms, usually in newborns. These signs and symptoms may include:

- Rapid breathing

- Cyanosis (a bluish tint to the skin, lips, and fingernails)

- Fatigue (tiredness)

- Poor blood circulation

Congenital heart defects don't cause chest pain or other painful symptoms.

Heart defects can cause heart murmurs (extra or unusual sounds heard during a heartbeat). Doctors can hear heart murmurs using a stethoscope. However, not all murmurs are signs of congenital heart defects. Many healthy children have heart murmurs.

Normal growth and development depend on a normal workload for the heart and normal flow of oxygen-rich blood to all parts of the body. Babies who have congenital heart defects may have cyanosis and tire easily while feeding. As a result, they may not gain weight or grow as they should.

Older children who have congenital heart defects may get tired easily or short of breath during physical activity.

Many types of congenital heart defects cause the heart to work harder than it should. With severe defects, this can lead to heart failure. Heart failure is a condition in which the heart can't pump enough blood to meet the body's needs. Symptoms of heart failure include:

- Shortness of breath or trouble breathing

- Fatigue with physical activity

- A buildup of blood and fluid in the lungs

- Swelling in the ankles, feet, legs, abdomen, and veins in the neck . . .

Treatment of Congenital Heart Defects

Although many children who have congenital heart defects don't need treatment, some do. Doctors repair congenital heart defects with catheter procedures or [open heart] surgery.

Sometimes doctors combine catheter and surgical procedures to repair complex heart defects, which may involve several kinds of defects. . . .

Some children who have complex congenital heart defects may need several catheter or surgical procedures over a period of years, or they may need to take medicines for years.

Catheter Procedures

Catheter procedures are much easier on patients than surgery. They involve only a needle puncture in the skin where the catheter (thin, flexible tube) is inserted into a vein or an artery.

Doctors don't have to surgically open the chest or operate directly on the heart to repair the defect(s). This means that recovery may be easier and quicker.

The use of catheter procedures has increased a lot in the past 20 years. They have become the preferred way to repair many simple heart defects, such as atrial septal defect (ASD) and pulmonary valve stenosis.

For ASD repair, the doctor inserts a catheter into a vein in the groin (upper thigh). He or she threads the tube to the heart's septum. A device made up of two small disks or an umbrella-like device is attached to the catheter.

When the catheter reaches the septum, the device is pushed out of the catheter. The device is placed so that it plugs the hole between the atria. It's secured in place and the catheter is withdrawn from the body.

Within 6 months, normal tissue grows in and over the device. The closure device does not need to be replaced as the child grows.

For pulmonary valve stenosis, the doctor inserts a catheter into a vein and threads it to the heart's pulmonary valve. A tiny balloon at the end of the catheter is quickly inflated to push apart the leaflets, or "doors," of the valve.

Then, the balloon is deflated and the catheter and balloon are withdrawn. This procedure can be used to repair any narrowed valve in the heart.

To help guide the catheter, doctors often use echocardiography (echo), transesophageal echo (TEE), and coronary angiography.

TEE is a special type of echo that takes pictures of the heart through the esophagus. The esophagus is the passage leading from the mouth to the stomach. Doctors also use TEE to examine complex heart defects.

Surgery

A child may need open-heart surgery if his or her heart defect can't be fixed using a catheter procedure. Sometimes one surgery can repair the defect completely. If that's not possible, the child may need more surgeries over months or years to fix the problem.

Cardiac surgeons may use open-heart surgery to:

- Close holes in the heart with stitches or a patch

- Repair or replace heart valves

- Widen arteries or openings to heart valves

- Repair complex defects, such as problems with the location of blood vessels near the heart or how they are formed

Rarely, babies are born with multiple defects that are too complex to repair. These babies may need heart transplants. In this procedure, the child's heart is replaced with a healthy heart from a deceased child. The heart has been donated by the deceased child's family.

Living with a Congenital Heart Defect

The outlook for children who have congenital heart defects is much better today than in the past. Advances in testing and treatment allow most of these children to survive to adulthood. They're able to live active, productive lives.

Many of these children need only occasional checkups with a cardiologist (heart specialist) as they grow up and go through adult life.

Children who have complex heart defects need long-term care from trained specialists. This will help them stay as healthy as possible and maintain a good quality of life.

| "[Lip and palate] clefts . . . are one of
  the most common birth defects."

Cleft Lip and Cleft Palate Are Common Birth Defects

Centers for Disease Control and Prevention

In the following viewpoint, the Centers for Disease Control and Prevention (CDC) contends that cleft lip and cleft palate are very common birth defects but are highly treatable. The CDC claims that ongoing studies are looking into the causes of orofacial (mouth and face) birth defects in an attempt to prevent them. According to the author, surgery is often the treatment for cleft lip and cleft palate. The CDC is one of the major operating components of the US Department of Health and Human Services, charged with creating the expertise, information, and tools that people and communities need to protect their health.

As you read, consider the following questions:

1. According to the CDC, how many babies in the United States are born with cleft palate each year?

2. What two risk factors does the author identify as having recently been found to increase the risk of orofacial clefts?

"Facts About Cleft Lip and Cleft Palate," Centers for Disease Control and Prevention, July 19, 2012.

3. According to the CDC, surgery to repair a cleft lip usually occurs at what age?

Cleft lip and cleft palate are birth defects that occur when a baby's lip or mouth do not form properly. Together, these birth defects commonly are called "orofacial clefts". These birth defects happen early during pregnancy. A baby can have a cleft lip, a cleft palate, or both.

Children with a cleft lip with or without a cleft palate or a cleft palate alone often have problems with feeding and talking. They also might have ear infections, hearing loss, and problems with their teeth.

The Incidence of Cleft Lip and Cleft Palate

The Centers for Disease Control and Prevention (CDC) recently estimated that each year 2,651 babies in the United States are born with a cleft palate and 4,437 babies are born with a cleft lip with or without a cleft palate. Cleft lip is more common than cleft palate. Isolated orofacial clefts, or clefts that occur with no other birth defects, are one of the most common birth defects in the United States. About 70% of all orofacial clefts are isolated clefts.

The lip forms between the fourth and seventh weeks of pregnancy. A cleft lip happens if the tissue that makes up the lip does not join completely before birth. This results in an opening in the upper lip. The opening in the lip can be a small slit or it can be a large opening that goes through the lip into the nose. A cleft lip can be on one or both sides of the lip or in the middle of the lip, which occurs very rarely. Children with a cleft lip also can have a cleft palate.

The roof of the mouth is called the "palate." It is formed between the sixth and ninth weeks of pregnancy. A cleft palate happens if the tissue that makes up the roof of the mouth does not join correctly. Among some babies, both the front and back parts of the palate are open. Among other babies, only part of the palate is open.

The Causes of Orofacial Clefts

Just like the many families affected by birth defects, CDC wants to find out what causes them. Understanding the risk factors that can increase the chance of having a baby with a birth defect will help us learn more about the causes. CDC currently [mid-2012] is working on one of the largest studies in the United States—the National Birth Defects Prevention Study—to understand the causes of and risk factors for birth defects. This study is looking at many possible risk factors for birth defects, such as orofacial clefts.

The causes of orofacial clefts among most infants are unknown. Some children have a cleft lip or cleft palate because of changes in their genes. Cleft lip and cleft palate are thought to be caused by a combination of genes and other factors, such as exposures in the environment, maternal diet, and medication use.

Recently, CDC reported on important findings about some factors that increase the risk of orofacial clefts:

- Smoking—Women who smoke during pregnancy are more likely to have a baby with an orofacial cleft than women who do not smoke.

- Diabetes—Women with diabetes diagnosed before pregnancy have been shown to be an increased risk of having a child with a cleft lip with or without cleft palate.

CDC continues to study birth defects, such as orofacial clefts and how to prevent them. If you smoke or have diabetes, and you are pregnant or thinking about becoming pregnant, talk with your doctor about ways to increase your chances of having a healthy baby.

Diagnosing Orofacial Clefts

Orofacial clefts sometimes can be diagnosed during pregnancy, usually by a routine ultrasound. Most often, orofacial clefts are diagnosed after the baby is born. However, sometimes minor clefts (e.g., submucous cleft palate and bifid uvula) might not be diagnosed until later in life.

Services and treatment for children with orofacial clefts can vary depending on the severity of the cleft; the presence of associated syndromes or other birth defects, or both; and the child's age and needs. Surgery to repair a cleft lip usually occurs in the first few months of life and is recommended within the first 12 months of life. Surgery to repair a cleft palate is recommended within the first 18 months of life. Many children will need additional surgeries as they get older. Although surgical repair can improve the look and appearance of a child's face, it also may improve breathing, hearing, speech, and language. Children born with orofacial clefts also might need different types of treatments and services, such as special dental or orthodontic care or speech therapy.

Because children and individuals with orofacial clefts often require a variety of services that need to be provided in a coordinated manner, services and treatment by cleft teams is recommended. Cleft teams provide a coordinated, interdisciplinary team approach to care for children with orofacial clefts. These teams usually consist of experienced and qualified physicians and health care providers from different specialties. Cleft teams and centers are located throughout the United States and other countries. Resources are available to help in choosing a cleft team. With treatment, most children with orofacial clefts do well and lead a healthy life.

❚ *"Down syndrome is a genetic condition that occurs in one in every 691 births."*

Down Syndrome Is a Common Chromosomal Birth Condition

National Down Syndrome Society

In the following viewpoint, the National Down Syndrome Society (NDSS) claims that Down syndrome is the most frequently occurring chromosomal birth defect. NDSS explains the differences among the different types of Down syndrome and how diagnosis for Down syndrome occurs, both pre- and post-natally. NDSS notes that although Down syndrome frequently puts people at risk for medical conditions, most people with Down syndrome live healthy, fulfilling lives. NDSS is a national organization that advocates for the value, acceptance, and inclusion of people with Down syndrome.

As you read, consider the following questions:

1. According to NDSS, approximately how many people in the United States have Down syndrome?

2. What percentage of children with Down syndrome are born to women under thirty-five years of age, according to the author?

3. Testing for Down syndrome with either chorionic villus sampling or amniocentesis carries what risk of miscarriage, according to the author?

Down syndrome is a genetic condition that occurs in one in every 691 births. It is the most frequently occurring chromosomal condition and is found in people of all races and economic levels. More than 400,000 people in the United States have Down syndrome. A few of the common physical traits of Down syndrome are low muscle tone, small stature, an upward slant to the eyes, and a single deep crease across the center of the palm. Every person with Down syndrome is a unique individual and may possess these characteristics to different degrees or not at all.

The Impact of Down Syndrome

People with Down syndrome have an increased risk for certain medical conditions such as congenital heart defects, respiratory and hearing problems, Alzheimer's disease, childhood leukemia, and thyroid conditions. However, many of these conditions are now treatable, so most people with Down syndrome lead healthy lives. Life expectancy for people with Down syndrome has increased dramatically in recent decades—from 25 [years] in 1983 to 60 today.

People with Down syndrome experience cognitive delays, but the effect is usually mild to moderate and is not indicative of the many strengths and talents that each individual possesses. Children with Down syndrome learn to sit, walk, talk, play, and do most other activities, only somewhat later than their peers without Down syndrome.

Quality educational programs, a stimulating home environment, good health care, and positive support from family, friends and the community enable people with Down syndrome to realize their life aspirations and lead fulfilling lives. People with Down syndrome attend school, work, participate in decisions that concern them, and contribute to society in many wonderful ways.

The Different Types of Down Syndrome

In every cell in the human body there is a nucleus, where genetic material is stored in genes. Genes carry the codes responsible for all of our inherited traits and are grouped along rod-like structures called chromosomes. Normally, the nucleus of each cell contains 23 pairs of chromosomes, half of which are inherited from each parent.

Down syndrome is usually caused by an error in cell division called "nondisjunction." Nondisjunction results in an embryo with three copies of chromosome 21 instead of the usual two. Prior to or at conception, a pair of 21st chromosomes in either the sperm or the egg fails to separate. As the embryo develops, the extra chromosome is replicated in every cell of the body. This type of Down syndrome, which accounts for 95% of cases, is called Trisomy 21.

The two other types of Down syndrome are called mosaicism and translocation. Mosaicism occurs when nondisjunction of chromosome 21 takes place in one—but not all—of the initial cell divisions after fertilization. When this occurs, there is a mixture of two types of cells, some containing the usual 46 chromosomes and others containing 47. Those cells with 47 chromosomes contain an extra chromosome 21. Mosaicism accounts for about 1% of all cases of Down syndrome. Research has indicated that individuals with mosaic Down syndrome may have fewer characteristics of Down syndrome than those with other types of Down syndrome. However, broad generalizations are not possible due to the wide range of abilities people with Down syndrome possess.

Translocation accounts for about 4% of all cases of Down syndrome. In translocation, part of chromosome 21 breaks off during cell division and attaches to another chromosome, typically chromosome 14. While the total number of chromosomes in the cells remain 46, the presence of an extra part of chromosome 21 causes the characteristics of Down syndrome.

The Cause of Down Syndrome

Regardless of the type of Down syndrome a person may have, all people with Down syndrome have an extra, critical portion of chromosome 21 present in all or some of their cells. This additional genetic material alters the course of development and causes the characteristics associated with Down syndrome.

The cause of nondisjunction is currently unknown, but research has shown that it increases in frequency as a woman ages. However, due to higher birth rates in younger women, 80% of children with Down syndrome are born to women under 35 years of age. There is no definitive scientific research that indicates that Down syndrome is caused by environmental factors or the parents' activities before or during pregnancy.

Once a woman has given birth to a baby with Trisomy 21, it is estimated that her chances of having another baby with Trisomy 21 is 1% greater than her chances by age alone. The age of the mother does not seem to be linked to the risk of translocation. Most cases are sporadic—that is, chance events. However, in about one third of cases, one parent is a carrier of a translocated chromosome. The risk of recurrence of translocation is about 3% if the father is the carrier and 10–15% if the mother is the carrier. Genetic counseling can determine the origin of translocation.

The Diagnosis of Down Syndrome

There are two types of tests for Down syndrome that can be performed before a baby is born: screening tests and diagnostic tests. Prenatal screens estimate the chance of the fetus hav-

Age and Down Syndrome

Maternal Age	Incidence of Down syndrome	Maternal Age	Incidence of Down syndrome
20	1 in 2,000	35	1 in 350
21	1 in 1,700	36	1 in 300
22	1 in 1,500	37	1 in 250
23	1 in 1,400	38	1 in 200
24	1 in 1,300	39	1 in 150
25	1 in 1,200	40	1 in 100
26	1 in 1,100	41	1 in 80
27	1 in 1,050	42	1 in 70
28	1 in 1,000	43	1 in 50
29	1 in 950	44	1 in 40
30	1 in 900	45	1 in 30
31	1 in 800	46	1 in 25
32	1 in 720	47	1 in 20
33	1 in 600	48	1 in 15
34	1 in 500	49	1 in 10

TAKEN FROM: National Down Syndrome Society, "The NDSS Brochure: An Overview of Down Syndrome and NDSS." www.ndss.org.

ing Down syndrome. These tests only provide a probability. Diagnostic tests can provide a definitive diagnosis with almost 100% accuracy.

Most screening tests involve a blood test and an ultrasound (sonogram). The tests (or serum screening tests) measure quantities of substances in the blood of the mother. Together with a woman's age, these are used to estimate her chance of having a child with Down syndrome. These blood tests are often performed in conjunction with a detailed sonogram to check for "markers" (characteristics that some researchers feel may have a significant association with Down syndrome). Recently, researchers have developed a maternal serum/ultrasound/age combination that yields higher accuracy at an earlier stage in the pregnancy. Still, the screen will not definitively diagnose Down syndrome.

Prenatal screening tests are now routinely offered to women of all ages. If the chance of having a child with Down syndrome is high from prenatal screening, doctors will often advise a mother to undergo diagnostic testing if they desire a definitive diagnosis. The diagnostic procedures available for prenatal diagnosis of Down syndrome are chorionic villus sampling (CVS) and amniocentesis. These procedures, which carry up to a 1% risk of causing a spontaneous termination (miscarriage), are practically 100% accurate in diagnosing Down syndrome. Amniocentesis is usually performed in the second trimester after 15 weeks of gestation, CVS in the first trimester between 9 and 11 weeks.

Down syndrome is usually identified at birth by physical traits: low muscle tone, a single deep crease across the palm of the hand, a slightly flattened facial profile and an upward slant to the eyes. These features may be present in babies without Down syndrome, therefore a karyotype chromosomal analysis is done to confirm the diagnosis. To obtain a karyotype, doctors draw blood to examine the cells. They photograph the chromosomes and group them by size, number, and shape. By examining the karyotype, doctors can diagnose Down syndrome. A similar genetic test called FISH [fluorescence in situ hybridization] can confirm a diagnosis in a shorter amount of time.

"Every day, about eight babies born in the United States have Spina Bifida or a similar birth defect of the brain and spine."

Spina Bifida Is a Common Birth Defect

Spina Bifida Association

In the following viewpoint, the Spina Bifida Association claims that there are several types of spina bifida, some of which are harmless and some of which are quite serious. The author contends that there are a variety of mental and social problems that accompany spina bifida but that the majority of those with spina bifida are of normal intelligence and are able to play sports, and they live to be adults. The Spina Bifida Association is a national voluntary health agency solely dedicated to enhancing the lives of those with spina bifida.

As you read, consider the following questions:

1. What is the most severe form of spina bifida, according to the author?

2. The Spina Bifida Association claims that what vitamin can help prevent spina bifida if taken by women before and during pregnancy?

3. What percentage of babies born with spina bifida will live to be adults, according to the Spina Bifida Association?

Spina Bifida literally means "split spine." Spina Bifida happens when a baby is in the womb and the spinal column does not close all of the way. Every day, about eight babies born in the United States have Spina Bifida or a similar birth defect of the brain and spine. . . .

Scientists believe that genetic and environmental factors act together to cause the condition.

The Different Types of Spina Bifida

Occult Spinal Dysraphism (OSD)

Infants with this have a dimple in their lower back. Because most babies with dimples do not have OSD, a doctor has to check using special tools and tests to be sure. Other signs are red marks, hyperpigmented patches on the back, tufts of hair or small lumps. In OSD, the spinal cord may not grow the right way and can cause serious problems as a child grows up. Infants who might have OSD should be seen by a doctor, who will recommend tests.

Spina Bifida Occulta

It is often called "hidden Spina Bifida" because about 15 percent of healthy people have it and do not know it. Spina Bifida Occulta [SBO; *occulta* means "hidden"] usually does not cause harm, and has no visible signs. The spinal cord and nerves are usually fine. People find out they have it after having an X-ray of their back. It is considered an incidental finding because the X-ray is normally done for other reasons. However, in a small group of people with SBO, pain and neurological symptoms may occur. Tethered cord can be an insidious complication that requires investigation by a neurosurgeon.

Spina Bifida in the United States

Spina bifida, which literally means "cleft spine," is characterized by the incomplete development of the brain, spinal cord, and/or meninges (the protective covering around the brain and spinal cord). It is the most common neural tube defect in the United States—affecting 1,500 to 2,000 of the more than 4 million babies born in the country each year. An estimated 166,000 individuals with spina bifida live in the United States.

National Institute of Neurological Disorders and Stroke, June 2013. www.ninds.nih.gov.

Meningocele

A meningocele causes part of the spinal cord to come through the spine like a sac that is pushed out. Nerve fluid is in the sac, and there is usually no nerve damage. Individuals with this condition may have minor disabilities.

Myelomeningocele (Meningomyelocele), also called Spina Bifida Cystica

This is the most severe form of Spina Bifida. It happens when parts of the spinal cord and nerves come through the open part of the spine. It causes nerve damage and other disabilities. Seventy to ninety percent of children with this condition also have too much fluid on their brains. This happens because fluid that protects the brain and spinal cord is unable to drain like it should. The fluid builds up, causing pressure and swelling. Without treatment, a person's head grows too big, and may have brain damage. Children who do not have Spina Bifida can also have this problem, so parents need to check with a doctor.

Treatment of Spina Bifida

A child with Meningomyelocele usually is operated on within two to three days of birth. This prevents infections and helps save the spinal cord from more damage.

A child with Meningocele usually has it treated with surgery, and more often than not, the child is not paralyzed. Most children with this condition grow up fine, but they should be checked by a doctor because they could have other serious problems, too.

A child with OSD should see a surgeon. Most experts think that surgery is needed early to keep nerves and the brain from becoming more damaged as the child grows.

Spina Bifida Occulta usually does not need to be treated.

Prevention of Spina Bifida

Women who are old enough to have babies should take folic acid before and during the first three months of pregnancy. Because half of the pregnancies in the United States are unplanned, the Spina Bifida Association asks women to take a vitamin with 400 mcg (0.4 mg) of folic acid each day during the years of their lives when they are possibly able to have children.

Women who have a child or sibling with Spina Bifida, have had an affected pregnancy or have Spina Bifida themselves should take 4000 mcg (4.0 mg) of folic acid for one to three months before and during the first three months of pregnancy.

Folic acid is a vitamin that the body needs to grow and be healthy. It is found in many foods, but the man-made or synthetic form in pills is actually better absorbed by our bodies.

Conditions Associated with Spina Bifida

Children and young adults with Spina Bifida can have mental and social problems. They also can have problems with walking and getting around or going to the bathroom, latex allergy, obesity, skin breakdown, gastrointestinal disorders, learning disabilities, depression, tendonitis and sexual issues.

People with Spina Bifida must learn how to get around independently, by using things like crutches, braces or wheelchairs. With help, it also is possible for children to learn how to go to the bathroom on their own. Doctors, nurses, teachers and parents should know what a child can and cannot do so they can help the child (within the limits of safety and health) be independent, play with kids that are not disabled and to take care of themselves.

Detection of Spina Bifida

There are three tests.[1]

1. A blood test during the 16th to 18th weeks of pregnancy. This is called the alpha-fetoprotein (AFP screening test). This test is higher in about 75–80% of women who have a fetus with Spina Bifida. AFP testing is not the most reliable form of detection, and is not frequently done anymore.

2. An ultrasound of the fetus. This is also called a sonogram and can show signs of Spina Bifida such as the open spine. This is the usual way that most SB pregnancies are detected.

3. A test where a small amount of the fluid from the womb is taken through a thin needle. This is called maternal amniocentesis and can be used to look at protein levels.

Management of Spina Bifida

With help, children with Spina Bifida can lead full lives. Most do well in school, and many play in sports. Because of today's

---

1. Parents should know that no medical test is perfect, and these tests are not always right.

medicine, about 90 percent of babies born with Spina Bifida now live to be adults, about 80 percent have normal intelligence and about 75 percent play sports and do other fun activities.

As type and level of severity differ among people with Spina Bifida, each person with the condition faces different challenges and may require different treatments.

The best way to manage Spina Bifida is with a team approach. Members of the team may include neurosurgeons, urologists, orthopedists, physical and occupational therapists, orthotists, psychologists and medical social workers.

| *"Congenital disorders are a common condition . . . worldwide."*

Birth Defects

World Health Organization

In the following viewpoint, the World Health Organization (WHO) argues that birth defects are an unacknowledged cause of mortality, disability, and negative social effects worldwide. The WHO contends that because birth defects themselves vary considerably in terms of cause and severity, prevention and treatment must be tailored to fit the situation in an attempt to reduce the negative impact of the defect. The WHO is a specialized agency of the United Nations that is concerned with international public health.

As you read, consider the following questions:

1. The World Health Organization estimates that how many deaths worldwide were caused by birth defects in 2004?

2. What four examples does the author give of public health approaches to preventing birth defects of environmental origin?

3. The author claims that what percentage of children with birth defects have a malformation of a single organ, system, or limb?

1. The report aims to inform the discussion on birth defects, including definition, epidemiology, burden of disease and interventions for prevention and care, as well as indications of how these interventions might be integrated into existing health services. An earlier version of this report was considered by the Executive Board at its 126th session,[1] following which the Board adopted resolution EB126.R6.

Definition

2. The International statistical classification of diseases and related health problems, tenth revision (ICD-10), includes birth defects in Chapter XVII: Congenital malformations, deformations and chromosomal abnormalities. Birth defects like inborn errors of metabolism and blood disorders of prenatal origin appear in other chapters. Birth defects can be defined as structural or functional abnormalities, including metabolic disorders, which are present from birth. The term congenital disorder is considered to have the same definition; the two terms are used interchangeably.[2] The eleventh revision of the classification provides an opportunity for a review of the current entry.

Irrespective of definition, birth defects can cause spontaneous abortions and stillbirths and are a significant but underrecognized cause of mortality and disability among infants and children under five years of age. They can be life-threatening, result in long-term disability, and negatively affect individuals, families, health-care systems and societies.

Birth Defects and Global Newborn and Child Mortality

4. Congenital disorders are a common condition. WHO estimates that some 260,000 deaths worldwide (about 7% of all

neonatal deaths) were caused by congenital anomalies in 2004.[3] They are most prominent as a cause of death in settings where overall mortality rates are lower, for example in the European Region, where as many as 25% of neonatal deaths are due to congenital anomalies.

5. There are currently no sound estimates of the number of children born with a serious congenital disorder attributable to genetic or environmental causes. The most common serious congenital disorders are congenital heart defects, neural tube defects and Down syndrome. Haemoglobinophathies (including thalassaemia and sickle-cell disease) and glucose-6-phosphate dehydrogenase deficiency, which are not covered by the ICD-10 definition of congenital anomalies, account for 6% of all congenital disorders.

6. Considerable uncertainties remain as to the incidence of and mortality attributable to congenital disorders, especially in countries that lack adequate registration of deaths. However, existing figures indicate that work on reducing the incidence of and mortality associated with congenital anomalies needs to be linked to efforts to achieve the Millennium Development Goal 4 target of a two thirds reduction in the mortality rate of children under five years of age between 1990 and 2015.

7. Birth defects are a diverse group of disorders of prenatal origin which can be caused by single gene defects, chromosomal disorders, multifactorial inheritance, environmental teratogens [causes of birth defects] and micronutrient deficiencies. Maternal infectious diseases such as syphilis and rubella are a significant cause of birth defects in low- and middle-income countries. Maternal illnesses like diabetes mellitus, conditions such as iodine and folic acid deficiency, and exposure to medicines and recreational drugs including alcohol and tobacco, certain environmental chemicals, and high doses of radiation are other factors that cause birth defects.

Prevention

8. The wide range of causes of birth defects means that a portfolio of prevention approaches is needed. Most birth defects of environmental origin can be prevented by public health approaches, including prevention of sexually transmitted infections, legislation controlling management of toxic chemicals (e.g. certain agricultural chemicals), vaccination against rubella, and fortification of basic foods with micronutrients (iodine and folic acid). Prevention may be considered in terms of life stage.

9. Preconception care aims to ensure the optimal physical and mental well-being of women and their partners at the onset of and during early pregnancy, to increase the likelihood of a normal pregnancy and the delivery of a healthy infant. It enables the timely deployment of primary prevention interventions which aim to prevent teratogen-induced birth defects (including those caused by congenital syphilis and rubella), defects caused by iodine deficiency disorder, neural tube defects (and possibly other malformations), and maternal-age-related chromosomal disorders (e.g. Down syndrome). The timely identification of a family risk of inherited disease, and carrier screening with genetic counselling, enable couples to limit family size where there is a known risk.

10. Prevention during pregnancy requires risk identification and management. Some of the interventions and services related to this can raise ethical, legal and social issues and may have cost implications. Such services include prenatal screening and diagnosis for birth defects, selective termination of pregnancy, and the availability of counselling services. Minimally invasive screening methods are currently available, such as taking maternal blood for the measurement of several metabolites in the maternal serum. Abnormal levels of biochemical markers are also associated with fetal structural defects such as Down syndrome, neural tube defects and open ventral wall defects. The detection rate of congenital disorders in the

first trimester through biochemical screening is improved when it is undertaken in tandem with ultrasound screening involving nuchal translucency and other ultrasonographical assessments. Ultrasonography in the second trimester is useful to detect major structural defects.

Detection, Treatment and Care

11. Screening of newborn infants for congenital disorders facilitates early detection, treatment and care. Neonatal screening programmes (physical examination of all neonates and screening for congenital hypothyroidism, phenylketonuria, sickle-cell disease and glucose-6-phosphate dehydrogenase deficiency) and training of primary health-care providers support the diagnosis and appropriate referral for treatment of infants with congenital disorders. Physical examination of all newborn infants by trained primary health-care practitioners is feasible in most health systems and allows the identification of many birth defects, including cardiovascular defects that are associated with a high risk of early mortality and referral.

12. Treatment of birth defects depends on the level of health care available. It comprises medical therapy, surgery, rehabilitation and palliative care when appropriate.

13. Effective life-saving medical treatment is available for several birth defects, including some common functional single-gene defects. Examples include treatment of neonatal jaundice in glucose-6-phosphate dehydrogenase deficiency and in Rhesus incompatibility, and therapy for congenital hypothyroidism, sickle-cell disorders, thalassaemia, haemophilia, cystic fibrosis, and other inborn errors of metabolism. Other treatment options include in utero therapy and postnatal surgical corrections; these are now under research and evaluation in a few selected centres for a number of conditions (e.g. congenital diaphragmatic hernia, congenital heart lesions, myelomeningocele, twin-to-twin transfusion syndrome).

14. Surgery is an important but largely unheralded component of the services required to treat children with birth defects. More than 60% of children with a birth defect have a congenital malformation of a single organ, system or limb. Many birth defects are amenable to cost-effective surgery that can be life-saving and improve long-term prognosis. Examples are surgery for simple congenital heart defects, cleft lip and palate, club foot, congenital cataracts, and gastrointestinal and urogenital abnormalities.

15. Appropriate treatment is also needed for impairments manifesting themselves after the neonatal period. This includes the early detection and treatment of physical, mental, intellectual or sensory impairments. Access to health and rehabilitation services is important to support the participation and inclusion of affected children.

16. With appropriate training, primary health-care practitioners can offer basic care for children with birth defects. They are able to recognize birth defects, diagnose common problems and identify associated disabilities, which in turn enables them to offer basic treatment and counselling, taking into account family and community circumstances and available medical services. Referral to specialist advice is considered when diagnosis is not possible at the primary health-care level.

Implications for Services

17. Services and interventions for the prevention and care of birth defects should be part of existing health-care services, in particular those concerned with maternal and child health. They should combine the best possible patient care with a preventive strategy encompassing education, pre-conception care, population screening, genetic counselling, and the availability of diagnostic services. That strategy must deliver services for the prevention and care of birth defects as part of a continuum of interventions for maternal and child health. De-

pending on countries' health-care capacities, these services should go beyond primary health care to include obstetric, paediatric, surgical, laboratory, radiological and, if available, clinical genetic services in secondary and tertiary health care.

18. Effective delivery of services for the prevention and care of birth defects depends on the availability of a range of specialist clinical and diagnostic services, and a primary health-care system that is able to use them. A nucleus of expertise in medical genetics, paediatric surgery, imaging, and fetal medicine is required, with the potential to expand to meet needs. Conventional laboratory services (haematological, microbiological, and biochemical) need to be supplemented with cytogenetic and DNA-based diagnostic services. Introduction may need to be a gradual process. Over time, the new technologies will support more efficient and cost-effective service delivery.

19. The diversity of priority conditions, social structures, cultural conventions and health-care capabilities means that countries need to be able to consider a range of possible services, assessing costs and relative effectiveness, in order to make a selection and decide the sequence of implementation. However, no organized guidance is yet available on this. The WHO Secretariat has an important potential role to play in identifying successful models, and providing coherent information on community genetics that is accessible to public health policy-makers.

Potential Actions

20. There are several country-level actions that can support the development of services for the prevention and care of birth defects. Prevention requires basic public health approaches to be integrated into health systems including maternal and child health services. Many of the services and interventions proposed are already within the reach of low- and middle-income countries while others can be added as needs and resources determine.

21. Basic components of a national programme for the prevention and care of birth defects include:

(a) commitment of policy-makers and provision of adequate managerial support;

(b) a core network of appropriate specialist clinical and laboratory services that can be expanded in response to demand;

(c) integration of approaches to the prevention and care of birth defects into primary health care, with an emphasis on maternal and child health;

(d) education and training for health-care providers, particularly those in primary health care;

(e) organization of health-education programmes for the general population and recognized high-risk groups;

(f) establishment of effective mechanisms to foster development of patient-parent support organizations, and collaboration with them in caring for people with birth defects and their families;

(g) definition of the ethical, legal, religious and cultural issues relevant to formulating services appropriate for the local population;

(h) initiation and monitoring of population-screening programmes such as screening of newborn infants, premarital/pre-pregnancy screening, and screening during pregnancy;

(i) establishment of appropriate surveillance systems for birth defects[4]

22. The establishment or strengthening of national programmes for the control of birth defects needs technical guidance, and in this regard there are several priority actions for the international community.

(a) Resolve currently divergent opinions on the health burden of both environmental and constitutional birth defects, using the revision of ICD-10 to draw on expert review of available data and to consider broadening the groups of conditions beyond those currently included in the classification of congenital anomalies.

(b) Promote legislation and public health activities to minimize exposure of the population, and particularly of pregnant women, to potentially teratogenic infections, chemicals and other environmental risk factors.

(c) Define effective community services, and support the integration of the prevention and care of birth defects into maternal and child health programmes. Support the provision to health ministries of an organized assessment of requirements and costs, and support them in choosing priorities.

(d) Identify successful models that can be applied in low- and middle-income countries.

(e) Facilitate and support international networking on birth defect prevention and care programmes, with an emphasis on developing common approaches, and optimizing instruments for information, education, cost analysis and surveillance, among others. Promote informatics approaches in view of their potential to support cost-effectiveness.

Action by the Health Assembly

23. The Health Assembly is invited to adopt the resolution recommended by the Executive Board in resolution EB126.R6.

Notes

1. See document EB126/2010/REC/2, summary record of the seventh meeting.

2. *Management of birth defects and haemoglobin disorders: report of a joint WHO–March of Dimes meeting, Geneva, Switzerland, 17–19 May 2006.* Geneva, World Health Organization, 2006.

3. *The global burden of disease: 2004 update.* Geneva, World Health Organization, 2008.

4. Support in establishing surveillance systems may be obtained by collaborating with existing birth defect surveillance systems, including the International Clearinghouse for Birth Defects Surveillance and Research, which includes the Latin American Collaborative Study of Congenital Malformations, the WHO-supported International Database of Craniofacial Anomalies, and the European Registration of Congenital Anomalies.

Periodical and Internet Sources Bibliography

The following articles have been selected to supplement the diverse views presented in this chapter.

American Heart Association	"The Impact of Congenital Heart Defects," April 5, 2012. www.heart.org.
Ajediran I. Bello, Augustine A. Acquah, Jonathan N.A. Quartey, and Anna Hughton	"Knowledge of Pregnant Women About Birth Defects," *BMC Pregnancy and Childbirth*, February 20, 2013.
Centers for Disease Control and Prevention	"Facts About Gastroschisis," March 26, 2013. www.cdc.gov.
Centers for Disease Control and Prevention	"Facts About Upper and Lower Limb Reduction Defects," February 25, 2011. www.cdc.gov.
KidsHealth	"Birth Defects," June 2010. www.kidshealth.org.
KidsHealth	"Congenital Heart Defects," January 2012. www.kidshealth.org.
Russell S. Kirby and Julianne S. Collins	"Birth Defects in the United States: A National Perspective on Surveillance, Epidemiology, and Public Health," *Birth Defects Research Part A: Clinical and Molecular Teratology*, December 2010.
March of Dimes	"Birth Defects: Clubfoot," January 2013. www.marchofdimes.com.
E. Albert Reece	"Diagnosing Birth Defects," *OB GYN News*, January 2011.
Mitchel L. Zoler	"Congenital Heart Disease Rate Pegged at 2 Million," *Internal Medicine News*, May 1, 2012.

OPPOSING
VIEWPOINTS®
SERIES

CHAPTER 2

What Causes Birth Defects?

Chapter Preface

Birth defects have genetic and environmental causes. Down syndrome is a chromosomal disorder, for instance, and sickle-cell anemia is a single-gene disorder. Both are birth defects with genetic causes and for that reason have the possibility of being identified through genetic testing. However, the vast majority of birth defects are believed to be caused by a combination of genetic and environmental factors or are due to multiple factors. Heart defects, neural tube defects, and cleft palate are among the birth defects that are believed to be due to multiple factors. Still, a percentage of birth defects are believed to be solely environmental in origin, caused by teratogens (things that cause birth defects) that interfere with proper fetal development, such as medications, radiation, lead, or maternal illness during pregnancy. An example of a known teratogen is thalidomide, a medication used in the 1950s and 1960s that led to birth defects in babies worldwide.

Thalidomide was created by a German pharmaceutical company in the 1950s as a sedative and later marketed as a remedy for morning sickness in pregnant women. In the late 1950s and early 1960s it was available in dozens of countries around the world under different brand names. The drug was approved for use in Germany, the United Kingdom, and Canada. In the United States, the US Food and Drug Administration refused approval of the drug until further studies were conducted, although some American physicians gave their patients thalidomide for clinical testing.

Within the first few years of the drug's use, in 1961, an Australian obstetrician noticed an increased number of deformed babies at his hospital, all born to mothers who had taken thalidomide. A German pediatrician publicized the birth of thousands of children in Germany exhibiting abnormal limb growth, which he believed was linked to the use of thalidomide. The drug was withdrawn from most countries by the end of 1961, although it remained available in Canada until early 1962. It is estimated that between ten thousand and twenty thousand babies worldwide were born with defects caused by thalidomide, the main symptom being phocomelia, or malformation of the limbs. Approximately half of the babies born with defects due to thalidomide did not survive. Those who did survive suffered missing or underdeveloped limbs, deformed eyes, deformed internal organs, and sometimes blindness or deafness.

The birth defects that resulted from the use of thalidomide by pregnant women raised awareness about the dangers of pharmaceuticals during pregnancy, prompting many countries to enact stricter rules for the testing and licensing of pharmaceuticals, especially for use by pregnant women. To prevent or reduce the incidence of birth defects, it is important to know what causes them. Identifying teratogens, in particular, is an important way to prevent pregnant women from ingesting substances—such as thalidomide—that have a high risk of causing birth defects. The viewpoints in this chapter debate the various causes of defects in newborn children.

| "The problem of birth defects is related to environmental pollution."

Environmental Pollution Can Cause Birth Defects

Christina Larson

In the following viewpoint, Christina Larson argues that recent studies performed in China show a correlation between increased environmental pollution and a higher incidence of birth defects. She contends that studies have shown a link between pollution from the burning of coal and neural tube and other birth defects. In addition, Larson claims that research has correlated general air pollution in countries other than China with poor birth outcomes and stunted intellectual development. Christina Larson is a Bloomberg Businessweek *contributor.*

As you read, consider the following questions:

1. What is the rate of neural tube defects in China's Shanxi Province, according to Larson?

2. According to the author, a study from China's Chong-qing municipality showed what difference between children born in 2002 and those born in 2005?

3. The author cites a study of urban air pollution and birth outcomes in nine countries, including what five countries she names?

After one particularly prolonged spell of smoggy Beijing air in late January [2013], the *Atlantic Monthly*'s James Fallows posted a provocative piece online titled, "China's Pollution: The Birth Defect Angle." In it, he quoted troubling anecdotal e-mails from readers suggesting that China's degraded environment was taking a heavy toll on the living and the unborn alike. Yet the short piece ended with a question, not a scientific conclusion: Do we know if prolonged exposure to polluted air, water, or food causes birth defects?

Pollution and Birth Defects

It turns out that several scientists, both inside and outside China, have been studying that question in recent years—and their answer is yes. That doesn't mean that every woman giving birth in a polluted environment, or every child born, will experience lasting health problems, but the trend lines across a population are clear. Depending on the level of pollution and the frequency of exposure, observed impacts range from a rise in severe congenital birth defects to a greater frequency of preterm births and low birth weights, correlated with increased risk for infant mortality and for diabetes and cardiovascular disease later in life.

Tong Zhu, now a Princeton Global Scholar, together with research partners at Peking University Health Science Center and the University of Texas at Austin, recently published results of a 10-year investigation of severe birth defects in one of China's most polluted regions: coal-rich and coal-darkened Shanxi province. Specifically, the team was investigating the alarming frequency of congenital neural tube defects, in which portions of an infant's brain, skull, or spine are missing or do not connect properly. Most babies born with this condition live only a few weeks.

In the U.S., for every 10,000 live births, there are 7.5 infants with neural tube defects. In Shanxi province, that number is 18 times higher: 140 infants. "We wanted to understand what's really behind the problem," says Tong, who previously worked at Peking University in Beijing. "We wanted to find out what chemicals caused this."

Over a 10-year period, the researchers gathered placentas from 80 stillborn or newborn infants in Shanxi with the disorder. Based on their analysis, they confirmed that those infants had been exposed in utero to significant levels of pesticides, industrial solvents, and especially polycyclic aromatic hydrocarbons (PAHs), which are released into the air when fossil fuels are burned. In Shanxi, the abundant coal is used for power plants as well as for home cooking and heating. "We found higher concentrations [of the chemicals] in the placentas of infants with the birth defects" than in other infants, explains Tong, who says there is a "clear association" between the environment the mother is exposed to and birth outcomes. Their findings appeared in the Aug. 2, 2011, issue of the *Proceedings of the National Academy of Sciences*.

The Importance of Policy Changes

Another significant study, published in the October 2008 issue of *Environmental Health Perspectives*, had a silver lining. Coauthors at Columbia University in New York, Chongqing University of Medical Sciences, Fudan University in Shanghai, and Shanghai Jiao Tong University studied two sets of women who delivered babies in a district of China's Chongqing municipality. A heavily polluting coal-fired power plant in the district was closed in the intervening period, allowing the researchers to compare the birth outcomes before and after its shutdown—and they found a notable difference.

"The fetus is extremely sensitive to exposure to toxic chemicals," says Frederica Perera, one of the study's authors and the director of the Columbia Center for Children's Envi-

Particulate Air Pollution, Average 2001–2006

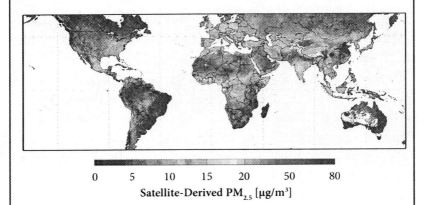

0   5   10   15   20   50   80

Satellite-Derived $PM_{2.5}$ [$\mu g/m^3$]

Source: Aaron van Donkelaar and Randall Martin at Dalhousie University, Halifax, Nova Scotia, Canada.

TAKEN FROM: Christina Larson, "Air Pollution, Birth Defects, and the Risk in China (and Beyond)," *Bloomberg Businessweek*, March 28, 2013. www.businessweek.com.

ronmental Health. "The organs and brain are rapidly developing, and the metabolic and DNA repair systems are not as efficient as in adults—there is less ability to clear out toxic chemicals."

The researchers enrolled two cohorts of nonsmoking mothers and newborns in 2002 and 2005. All the women lived within 2 kilometers of the site of Tongliang power plant, which was closed in 2004. Samples of umbilical cord blood were collected at the time of delivery and analyzed to record the presence of PAHs, mercury, and lead. The children were followed until their second birthday, when standardized tests known as Gesell Developmental Schedules were given to assess their behavioral and intellectual development. The children born in 2002, when the power plant was still operating, on average showed developmental delays, especially in motor skills.

Those born in 2005 did not exhibit the same setbacks. "It's actually a good-news story," says Perera. "The government shut down the power plant, and you could see immediate improvements" in child and maternal health. The takeaway, she emphasizes, is that policy changes can have swift impact.

Air Pollution and Birth Outcomes

While China attracts frequent headlines for its smoggy skies, it's hardly the only country where air pollution is a concern. A study published in the March 2013 issue of *Environmental Health Perspectives* looked at urban air pollution and birth outcomes in nine countries, including the U.S., South Korea, Brazil, Spain, and Italy. The authors examined 3 million total birth records.

The researchers established a correlation between elevated levels of particulate air pollution and elevated numbers of babies delivered at low birth weights in each of the 14 cities in 9 countries studied. They found a correlation between low birth weight and high PM 10 levels (particulate matter less than 10 micrometers in diameter), and separately, a similar correlation with high PM 2.5 levels (particulate matter less than 2.5 micrometers in diameter). For instance, each increase in PM 10 of 10 micrograms per cubic meter was associated with a 3 percent increase in babies with low birth weight. "On an individual level, the risk per person is perhaps not so great, but on a population level—when you consider hundreds of thousands of people impacted—it's very significant and costly for a government and health-care system to manage" the long-term health implications, says lead author Payam Dadvand of the Centre for Research in Environmental Epidemiology in Barcelona, Spain. Their study did not include research sites in China, where air pollution levels are generally higher than in the nine countries studied.

For a useful global comparison, researchers at Canada's Dalhousie University have used NASA [National Aeronautics and Space Administration] satellite data on air pollution—yes, aerosols can be detected from space—to create a color-coded world map showing average PM 2.5 levels for the years 2001–06. Northern China—including the cities Beijing and Tianjin and adjacent provinces Hebei and Shanxi—is not the world's only air-pollution hot spot, but it's among the most consistently hazardous.

Some Chinese officials have recently begun to discuss the problem. The director of the family planning agency in Shanxi province [An Huanxiao], where Princeton's Tong examined neural tube defects, told *China Daily* in 2009: "The problem of birth defects is related to environmental pollution, especially in eight main coal zones." Hu Yali, a professor at Nanjing University, estimated that pollution accounted for 10 percent of birth defects in China. The vice-minister of China's national family-planning ministry [Jiang Fan], which is now being folded into the health ministry, told *China Daily*, "The number of newborns with birth defects is constantly increasing in both urban and rural areas." Quite often, China's most polluted regions, including Shanxi, are among its poorest—local parents have scant resources to care for healthy or sick children.

> *"To find a chemical culprit for the birth defects would require not just identifying substances in the air, water, or soil that are capable of causing such defects, but also tracing their pathway to townspeople's bodies."*

Proving That Environmental Pollution Causes Birth Defects Is Difficult

Jacques Leslie

In the following viewpoint, Jacques Leslie claims that it is challenging to definitively link environmental pollutants with particular incidents of birth defects. Through telling the story about a rise in birth defects in Kettleman City, California, Leslie contends that because of the multiple environmental pollutants in the area and the small size of the population, it would be almost impossible to trace a birth defect back to any particular pollutant, even if some pollutants are in fact causing birth defects. Leslie is a journalist and author.

Jacques Leslie, "What's Killing the Babies of Kettleman City?," *Mother Jones*, vol. 35, no. 4, July–August 2010. Copyright © 2010, Foundation for National Progress. Reproduced by permission.

As you read, consider the following questions:

1. According to the author, residents of Kettleman City claim that over a three-year period recently, how many babies were born with serious birth defects?

2. The hazardous waste dump near Kettleman City accepted how many tons of hazardous waste in 2009, according to Leslie?

3. The author gives what examples of things that the cumulative impacts approach to environmentally vulnerable areas takes into account?

The first baby's name was America. She was born in September 2007, with Down syndrome, two heart murmurs, and part of her upper lip missing. She couldn't suck from a nipple, so her mother, Magdalena Romero, would stay up through the night to feed her with a special tube. America showed pleasure in music and delighted in being held by her four siblings. Magdalena thinks they felt a special tenderness for her because of her vulnerability.

A Rise in Birth Defects

Hospital officials told Magdalena that the baby wouldn't live a year, but she didn't want to believe it. Then, one morning when America was nearly five months old, her lips turned purple. Concluding that paramedics would consider a rescue futile, Magdalena drove the baby to the hospital herself and insisted that all efforts be made to save her. For a few days, America survived, tethered to machines. Then she died in her mother's arms.

A few flowers struggle to grow in the tiny patch of soil in front of the Romeros' house in Kettleman City, California, a farmworker community halfway between Los Angeles and San Francisco. Outside, the powder blue trim is peeling; inside, the house looks sparse, unfinished, except for an alcove off the living room that has become a memorial to America. On the wall hangs a carefully embroidered cloth with her name and birth date in red script and her tiny hand- and footprints rendered in pink; rosary beads are draped over the frame. Nearby, three photos of America sit atop a VCR—they're typical baby pictures, filled with pink and lace, that startle because of America's missing lip. Magdalena stands in front of the shrine; her lips form a slight smile, but her eyes look uncertain. "You feel all the time, every hour, that something is missing," she says. Magdalena, now 33, dared to have another child, whom she also named America. The toddler is healthy, but Alondra, her six-year-old sister, keeps asking, "Is this baby going to die too?"

There are between 30 and 64 births each year in Kettleman City. In 15 of the 22 years since California's public health department began tracking birth defects, all babies in the town were healthy, and in five other years, only one birth defect occurred. But in the last two years and 10 months [beginning in late 2007], residents say, at least 11 babies have been born with serious birth defects. Three eventually died; another was stillborn. Most have cleft lips or palates, and some have other, graver maladies. "When my child was born," Magdalena says, "I thought she was the only one with a deformity. But when it began happening to other babies, I realized there was something abnormal in my community."

A Small Town

Kettleman City—a dot on the map so insignificant that it is technically not even a town but a "census-designated place"— rose out of the scrublands of the western San Joaquin Valley in the late 1920s, following the discovery of oil in the nearby Kettleman Hills. The second-longest street in town, all half a mile of it, is named General Petroleum Avenue, and the third-longest is Standard Oil Avenue. Those names are as close to wealth as the town gets. Nearly half its 1,500 residents live below the poverty line, according to the 2000 census. A couple of miles south on Highway 41, at the junction with Interstate 5, sits an agglomeration of motels, gas stations, an In-N-Out Burger, and a Starbucks, but the town itself has no pharmacy, high school, or movie theater. It also lacks sidewalks, a supermarket, and a clean drinking-water supply (though the 444-mile California Aqueduct, which conveys water from the Sierras to dozens of Southern California cities, runs just past its border). Most Kettleman families travel 32 miles to Hanford, the county seat, to shop for food and bottled water.

Kettleman City does have a few convenience and liquor stores, three well-attended churches (Catholic, evangelical, and Pentecostal), and one tiny restaurant, La Perla, where the most popular menu item is a $3 burrito. Then again, popularity at La Perla is a relative concept; on most days it attracts only five or six patrons. Many families hail from the same Mexican town—La Piedad, in the state of Michoacán. Many have lived in Kettleman City for three generations; others arrived in the last few years. Maricela Mares-Alatorre, a 38-year-old teacher in a GED [high school diploma] program for farmworkers, is one of a tiny number of residents with a college degree. She describes Kettleman City as having "a Mayberry feeling with a Latino twist—that's why I stay. Even if I left, that doesn't mean the problems get solved. There are still vulnerable people here who can't speak for themselves, and we're supposed to abandon them?"

The "problems" are not just the recent wave of birth defects, but the many possible explanations for it, and, most worrisome of all, the prospect that the reason will never be identified. That uncertainty—which no one quite wants to admit—hovers over the town like smog.

The Toxins in Town

Despite Kettleman City's remote setting amid almond groves and tomato fields, its residents are exposed to a startling array of toxic chemicals. Nearly 100 trucks spewing diesel fumes roll through town daily on Highway 41, and many more come by on Interstate 5. More than half of Kettleman City's labor force consists of farmworkers who are routinely exposed to toxic pesticides, and residents can smell the chemicals sprayed on the fields that border the town on three sides. Kettleman City's two municipal wells are contaminated with naturally occurring arsenic and benzene. And there are projects in the works to build a massive natural gas power plant nearby, as well as to deposit 500,000 tons per year of Los Angeles sewage sludge on farmland a few miles from the town.

But the biggest environmental villain, in the view of local residents, is Waste Management Inc., which operates a vast hazardous-waste dump three miles from town. Waste Management is the nation's largest waste-disposal company, and the Kettleman Hills landfill is the biggest toxic-waste dump west of Alabama, where another Waste Management facility is located in another poor, minority community. California's two other toxic-waste dumps are also located near Latino farmworker towns.

Last year [2009] the Kettleman site accepted 356,000 tons of hazardous waste, consisting of tens of thousands of chemical compounds including asbestos, pesticides, caustics, petroleum products, and about 11,000 tons of materials contaminated with PCBs—now-banned chemicals linked to cancer and birth defects. Waste Management has been seeking permission since 2006 to increase the dump's size by nearly 50 percent.

A Fight Against Expansion

Kettleman City residents have been fighting that proposal, as they've fought other Waste Management projects over the years. In the early 1990s, the town became something of a cause célèbre when it resisted plans to build a toxic-waste incinerator at the dump. (Waste Management ended up withdrawing its application.)

Among the organizers in that case was Bradley Angel, a 56-year-old Long Island–reared Greenpeace activist who went on to run a San Francisco–based environmental nonprofit called Greenaction for Health and Environmental Justice. Angel continued to follow events in Kettleman, and in 2007, after a battle over Waste Management's application to continue storing PCBs at Kettleman Hills, he proposed doing a health survey of the town. Greenaction workers and two local environmental groups devised a 36-question survey and started knocking on doors.

What Angel expected to find was an abundance of cancer and asthma, diseases that are found at higher rates in places with substantial air pollution and that are prevalent in Kettleman City. But by the time volunteers had spoken to about 200 residents, they'd learned that five babies born over a 14-month period had cleft palates and other serious birth defects, and three of those babies had died. Since they'd counted only about 25 births during that period, they believed they had uncovered a stunningly large birth-defect cluster. Angel considered the findings so alarming that in 2008 he called off the survey to focus on publicizing the birth defects.

For many months, he got no traction. Government and Waste Management officials repeatedly dismissed his calls for a state investigation of the birth defects. Dr. Benjamin Hoffman, Waste Management's chief medical officer, told the *Hanford Sentinel* in July 2009, "I'll make a guess that you'll not find that cluster, that it doesn't exist . . . There are some birth defects, but I'm going to bet there's no unifying cause." Three months later, Kings County health officer Michael MacLean testified at a county planning commission meeting "If the United States doesn't know what causes most birth defects, what do you think is the probability that we're going to figure this out in [these] cases? We will only find what might possibly have caused this. We're going to end up with the same thing we started with."

The culture clash between Kettleman City's farmworkers and the white ranchers who hold power in Kings County was on full display at a Board of Supervisors meeting to consider Waste Management's application in December [2009]. About 150 Kettleman City residents rode buses chartered by activist groups to attend the meeting in Hanford. They were greeted by a few dozen police, including a K-9 unit, and a few hundred Waste Management employees dressed in green company T-shirts, who filled the rear third of the auditorium. The Kettleman residents who testified were alternately angry, respectful, dignified, and profane. "We're people just like you," said 15-year-old Miguel Alatorre, leader of a youth group that helped conduct the health survey. "We're not dogs . . . We're tired of all this dumping and toxic waste. We want it out." The supervisors listened impassively.

Some Government Response

It wasn't until the campaign yielded a few newspaper stories that officials started to pay attention. In December, the Board of Supervisors voted for a state investigation into the cluster. But a week later, it also unanimously approved Waste Management's expansion application. When I asked supervisor Joe Neves whether Kettleman City's health problems ought to rule out the dump's expansion, he seemed to view the question as an attack on modernity itself. "Does that mean that we shouldn't be growing crops?" he asked. "Does that mean we should just let everything go back to nature?"

In truth, the approval was likely motivated by more practical concerns. Under California law, county governments can tax dumps by as much as 10 percent of their revenue from hazardous waste; Waste Management's "franchise taxes" to Kings County amounted to more than $1.6 million last year [2009], and the company paid another $380,000 in property tax, making it one of the county's largest taxpayers. The expansion application still needed signoffs from several other government agencies, but Angel's threat to tie up the permit in appeals was starting to hint of futility. Meanwhile, Kettleman City residents kept reporting more birth defects; by last spring, Angel was counting 11.

Then the activists got a break. Angel had been lobbying the [President Barack] Obama-appointed regional EPA [Environmental Protection Agency] director, Jared Blumenfeld, and in January Blumenfeld announced his office would review its monitoring of the waste dump. (Blumenfeld also visited Kettleman City and met with the mothers.) Three days later, Gov. Arnold Schwarzenegger announced that the state Department of Public Health would investigate the birth defects. Soon afterward, an EPA spokesman said the agency wouldn't approve Waste Management's application "unless we are confident that the facility does not present a health risk to the community." California Sens. Barbara Boxer and Dianne Feinstein called for a moratorium on the expansion and sought federal funds for a water-treatment plant that would end the town's reliance on contaminated well water. At least for the time being, all this has given the people of Kettleman City hope.

The Difficulty in Proving Causation

The trouble is that science is not likely to back them up. To find a chemical culprit for the birth defects would require not just identifying substances in the air, water, or soil that are capable of causing such defects, but also tracing their pathway to townspeople's bodies. The odds of achieving either are low. For one thing, Kettleman City isn't big enough to support meaningful epidemiological statistics. Scientists know relatively little about how individual chemicals affect health, and next to nothing about their effects in combination. Kettleman City exists within such a thick chemical soup that it would be hard to identify an individual substance as the culprit—and the precise combination of exposures could be different for each family. Dr. Rick Kreutzer, who heads California's Division of Environmental and Occupational Disease Control, says that even though the most common defect is a cleft palate, the differences in the other defects indicate that there is no single cause. "We don't really expect that we're going to find that one big thing," he says.

Even more confounding, clusters—of birth defects, cancers, and other health problems—are not necessarily evidence of environmental harm. Richard Jackson, chairman of the environmental health sciences department at the University of California–Los Angeles and a leader in the creation of California's first birth-defect monitoring program, says "hard-learned experience" has taught him that "clusters are a statistical inevitability . . . If you throw a bunch of beans on a tile floor, some tiles are going to have five beans, and a bunch of them are going to have none." Kettleman City's accumulation of birth defects could be the result of nothing more than chance—though that possibility dwindles with each new case. Heredity, diet, and lifestyle could also play a part.

The Cumulative Impacts Approach

In the face of all this uncertainty, some scientists are arguing for a new approach to environmentally vulnerable areas called "cumulative impacts." They maintain that since chemical-by-chemical health studies don't reflect real-world circumstances, it makes sense to think more broadly, taking into account everything from polluted air and water to poverty, poor health care, and proximity to hazardous facilities.

"We think of biology more as a network now," says Amy D. Kyle, a University of California–Berkeley public health researcher and cumulative-impacts advocate. "There are lots of things going in your body at the same time, things get turned on and off, they can be interfered with to varying degrees by different chemical stressors. It's not like a road from A to B—it's more like traffic. If you have a crash, it doesn't stop all traffic. The whole system readjusts itself in ways that aren't linear. [In biology], the outcome depends on what else is going on—how old you are and what your other susceptibilities are, and the likelihood that multiple things can perturb these same pathways is greater than what we thought."

What this means for scientists and regulators, Kyle says, is that "we ought to think about more than one environmental factor at a time. That's different from the current paradigm, [where] policies are addressed at one pollutant at a time. When you get out into communities and you look around, and you see hazardous wastes, less health care, lead paint in their houses, you can't really think that that collection of environmental factors and [individual] sensitivities don't often matter. It's not really scientifically believable."

Rachel Morello-Frosch, an environmental health researcher at UC-Berkeley, calls Kettleman City "a poster child for cumulative impacts" because residents' health is compromised in so many ways. "Waste Management needs to be aware that its operations are adding to an already burdened community," she says. "The facility can't just pretend it's operating in a vacuum."

In the absence of a cumulative-impacts analysis—something that has yet to be attempted by any regulator anywhere in the US—Kettleman City is now the subject of a state-run epidemiological investigation, almost certainly a bittersweet accomplishment. The likeliest outcome—continued uncertainty about the birth defects' cause—could in fact help Waste Management by reinforcing its contention that no harm from the dump has been shown.

The Impact of a Study

Jackson concedes that in Kettleman City, where "there's no way the public will be satisfied without a serious investigation," an epidemiological study is required—but that doesn't mean it will have any meaningful impact. "Communities are often led to believe that a scientific investigation will lead to some answers," Jackson says. "But my own experience is that oftentimes an enormous amount of resources is put into an investigation, and at the end of it we really don't know much more than we did at the beginning, except that we now know the residents have terrible medical care, terrible dental care, the kids are way behind in school, they're way behind in immunizations and nutrition." In some ways, he argues, spending money "to give them an epidemiological study rather than care is really not the right thing to do."

Yet even if the study does not identify a culprit, the attention on Kettleman City still may yield benefits, such as the increasing likelihood that the federal government will fund a water-treatment plant for the town. And the federal investigation of the Waste Management dump may yet lead to tighter monitoring of the facility; this spring [2010], the probe turned up violations in handling PCBs. In response to the revelations, Waste Management issued a press release asserting that the chemicals were at "very low levels" and that "the health and safety of Kettleman City residents . . . are our highest priority." (The company says the contamination has since been cleaned up.)

But try telling that to 26-year-old Maura Alatorre, whose second child, Emmanuel, was born in May 2008 with numerous problems, including a cleft lip and an enlarged head. Surgery corrected some of the problems, but he continues to have allergies so severe that his doctor prescribed medication usually reserved for older children. He's had a seizure, and his parents have been told to expect many more because of his most serious problem, a defect in his corpus callosum—a vital portion of the brain that orchestrates communication between its two hemispheres. Emmanuel's right side lags behind his left, and he is likely to face intellectual deficiencies as he grows. Despite all this, he looks lively and curious and has clearly overcome some of his maladies. "God has made a miracle of my child," Maura says, sitting on her living room sofa with a smiling Emmanuel on her lap, "but I don't want to take the risk of having another one."

> "*[Research] that looked at a group of IVF kids with birth defects could not find evidence that the IVF lab procedures were the cause.*"

Assisted Reproduction Is Not a Significant Risk for Birth Defects

Ronald Bailey

In the following viewpoint, Ronald Bailey argues that there is not sufficient evidence to support having prospective parents rethink assisted reproduction because of the risk of birth defects. Bailey contends that although a recent study found a small increase in the incidence of birth defects in children born from the use of in vitro fertilization (IVF) and intracytoplasmic sperm injection (ICSI), the risk is incredibly small and does not pose an ethical challenge for people who want to use IVF and ICSI. Bailey is a science correspondent at Reason *magazine and author of* Liberation Biology: The Scientific and Moral Case for the Biotech Revolution.

Ronald Bailey, "Is Assisted Reproduction Too Risky for Kids?," *Reason.com*, May 1, 2012. Copyright © 2013 by Reason Magazine and Reason.com. All rights reserved. Reproduced by permission.

As you read, consider the following questions:

1. Bailey discusses a study finding the risk of birth defects to be what percentage higher in children born using assisted reproductive technologies?

2. Bailey claims that the increased risk of birth defects in children born using IVF and ICSI affected how many more children out of a hundred than did conception without these technologies?

3. According to the author, do the studies monitoring children born using IVF generally raise concerns?

Children conceived by means of some assisted reproductive technologies (ART) run a higher risk of being born with birth defects than do children conceived spontaneously, according to a new study in the journal *Fertility and Sterility*.

This has provoked some handwringing by University of Pennsylvania bioethicist Arthur Caplan, who observes that the study "showed large increase in the risk of having a child with a birth defect. The risk was 37 percent higher than that seen in children made the old fashioned way. That is a huge number." Caplan adds, "The large risk factor now on the table needs to be a key part of how everyone thinks about making babies in medical settings."

The researchers looked at the rate of birth defects reported in 46 studies of children born using regular in vitro fertilization (IVF) producing embryos by exposing eggs in a lab dish to sperm and then transferring them to a womb and intracytoplasmic sperm injection (ICSI) in which a single sperm is injected directly into an egg. The studies encompassed the births of just under 125,000 children worldwide. The researchers also wanted to see if there was any difference in the birth defect rates between regular IVF and ICSI. They did not find much difference in the rate of birth defects between the two assisted reproductive techniques.

Prior studies have also found an increase in birth defects among children born by means of assisted reproduction. So what is the magnitude of the risks? I am a bit puzzled about the way that Caplan characterized the results of the new study. What the researchers actually report is an increase in the relative risk of IVF and ICSI birth defects compared to the risk of birth defects among children born through what the fertility gurus label "spontaneous" conception. In the United States the rate of birth defects among children born by spontaneous means is about 3 out of 100. What does a 37 percent increase in birth defects among IVF babies represent? Basically, it means that the researchers found that 4 out of 100 IVF babies are born with birth defects. That is not nothing, but it sure does sound less scary than a 37 percent increase.

An Insignificant Issue

How to account for this reported increase in birth defects associated with assisted reproduction? The researchers note that the defects could be due to the underlying infertility of couples seeking treatment. For example, one study found that children born to subfertile couples (often defined as those who took longer than one year to conceive) have a higher rate of birth defects. It is also possible that the laboratory handling of eggs and sperm and embryos somehow damages them and thus increases the risk of birth defects. However, one study that looked at a group of IVF kids with birth defects could not find evidence that the IVF lab procedures were the cause. And it may be that closer scrutiny of children born by means of ART [assisted reproductive technologies] results in a higher reported rate of birth defects, thus misleadingly boosting the apparent relative risk.

Based on this study, Caplan asserts, "We need to be sure that long-term monitoring of children born by means of infertility treatment is routine and that more research is done into the causes of health problems for kids who cannot make choices about facing risk." First, as far as I can tell most studies that have monitored IVF kids are reassuring. For example, a 2010 follow up study of IVF kids up to grade 12 reported, "IVF children scored higher on standardized tests than their matched peers, suggesting that IVF does not have a negative effect on cognitive development." An earlier study had suggested that children conceived using IVF were taller than spontaneously conceived children. However, a subsequent study found no such difference.

Look, if these data stand up, then of course people who are considering using IVF should be told about the increased risks to their potential children. But how likely is it that parents would decide not to risk having a kid because there is a 3 percent chance they would suffer from a significant birth defect? That's the normal risk that any parent and any would-be kid face now. So raise the chance to 4 percent. How many people would change their minds about having a kid because of that increased risk? I suspect not too many.

Consequently, I am not quite sure what to make of Caplan's ominous assertion that seems to suggest that the risks faced by kids born via assisted reproduction are somehow more ethically significant than the risks faced by children born by conventional means. Nobody gets to choose who their parents are or what their characteristics will be before birth. ART and spontaneously conceived kids stand in exactly the same ethical relation to their parents with regard to the risks of being born.

| "The [antibiotics] sulfonamides and ni-
trofurantoins were associated with several birth defects."

The Use of Certain Antibiotics During Pregnancy May Cause Birth Defects

Jeffrey T. Jensen

In the following viewpoint, Jeffrey T. Jensen claims that a 2010 study shows an association between the use of two kinds of antibiotics and a variety of birth defects. Jensen notes that it is difficult to draw conclusions about causation from the type of study performed, a case-control study, but he cautions doctors against prescribing the named antibiotics to pregnant women just to be safe. Jensen is the Leon Speroff Professor of Obstetrics and Gynecology at Oregon Health and Science University in Portland and the editor of OB/GYN Clinical Alert.

As you read, consider the following questions:

1. In the study the author discusses, at what point in their pregnancies did the women studied use antibiotics?

2. Jensen cautions that case-control studies cannot establish causation, but he says they are able to serve what important role?

3. What three classes of antibiotics are most commonly used and not associated with birth defects in the study, according to the author?

The purpose of the National Birth Defects Prevention Study (NBDPS), published in the *Archives of Pediatric and Adolescent Medicine* (2009;163:978–85) was to estimate the association between antibacterial medications and selected birth defects. The authors conducted a population-based, multisite, case-control study of women who had pregnancies affected by 1 of more than 30 eligible major birth defects identified via birth defect surveillance programs. The study population included 13,155 cases of women with affected pregnancies and 4,941 control women with unaffected pregnancies randomly selected from the same geographical regions (10 states). The main exposure was reported maternal use of antibacterials (1 month before pregnancy through the end of the first trimester), and odds ratios (ORs) measuring the association between antibacterial use and selected birth defects were constructed and adjusted for potential confounders. The reported use of antibacterials increased during pregnancy, peaking during the third month.

Antibiotics Associated with Birth Defects

Sulfonamides were associated with anencephaly, hypoplastic left heart syndrome, coarctation of the aorta, choanal atresia, transverse limb deficiency, and diaphragmatic hernia.

Nitrofurantoins were associated with anophthalmia or microphthalmos, hypoplastic left heart syndrome, atrial septal defects and cleft lip with cleft palate.

Other antibacterial agents were not associated with a significant increase in the AOR [adjusted odds ratio] of these birth defects. The authors concluded that sulfonamides and nitrofurantoins were associated with several birth defects, indicating a need for additional scrutiny. In contrast, penicillins, erythromycins, and cephalosporins appeared to be safer alternatives.

The Usefulness of Case-Control Studies

The NBPS is conducted by investigators at the Centers for Disease Control and Prevention. This large representative multistate database is about as good as we get in the current United States health care system to assess exposure and rare outcomes in a large population-based classic case-control study. While case-control studies cannot demonstrate a causal relationship, they can suggest important relationships worthy of additional consideration. For the assessment of rare outcomes where prospective randomized studies are impractical, they provide the best evidence for clinical guidance.

This study received little press in the obstetric literature. As I discovered recently that nurses and residents at my institution were not aware of these results, I felt it was important to bring them to the attention of readers of *OB/GYN Clinical Alert*.

Case-control studies are always subject to confounding. Common events like urinary tract infections (UTIs) will lead to multiple exposures, and common drugs will be widely used. Recall bias further complicates studies of exposure, as those women that experience an abnormal pregnancy may have a greater tendency to report exposure or to recall the drug they were treated with.

The Advice for Doctors

More than 2% of women in this study were treated for a UTI in the first trimester. The authors designed their assessment to critical exposure during the period of early fetal development. Still, many of the abnormalities are restricted to an even more limited time of exposure, with most structural anomalies oc-

FDA Drug Risk Categories

Under the current system, the US Food and Drug Administration defines risk categories (A, B, C, D, X) for all drugs based on the level of risk the drug poses to the fetus and the nature of evidence supporting that risk assessment. The categories are as follows: (A) controlled studies do not demonstrate a risk to the human fetus; (B) animal studies do not show risk (no controlled studies in humans), or animal studies have shown adverse effect but controlled studies in humans show no risk; (C) animal studies have shown an adverse effect on the fetus (no controlled studies in humans); (D) investigational studies have shown evidence of human fetal risk; and (X) the drug is contraindicated.

*Krista S. Crider, et al., "Antibacterial Medication
Use During Pregnancy and Risk of Birth Defects
National Birth Defects Prevention Study,"*
Archives of Pediatrics and Adolescent Medicine,
vol. 163, no. 11, November 2, 2009.

curring before 6 weeks of gestation. The majority of subjects in the NBPS were treated between 8-13 weeks, well after the expected developmental critical windows for the listed anomalies.

However, the most commonly used antibiotics—penicillins, erythromycins, and cephalosporins (all FDA [Food and Drug Administration] pregnancy category B)—were not associated with an increased risk of anomalies in this study, while both nitrofurantoin and sulfonamides were associated with significant increased AOR of risk for a variety of anomalies. Sulfonamides (FDA pregnancy category C or D) have been shown to be teratogenic in animal studies, although it is unclear whether sulfonamides without trimethoprim pose a significant risk. The two drugs act synergistically to block two steps in the biosynthesis of reduced folates, and other case-control studies have demonstrated an increased risk of anomalies with first trimester exposure. These drugs can also affect bilirubin [a product of red blood cell breakdown that causes a yellow tint] metabolism and should not be used in the third trimester and while breast feeding. The observed increase in risk with nitrofurantoin (Category B) is more surprising. The drug primarily concentrates in the urinary tract and has not previously been associated with fetal harm. It is well tolerated, easy to take, and highly effective against most pathogens.

Taken together, the results from this study are far from conclusive. Still, this information will be available on the internet and your patients will be searching that source as soon as they leave the office with your prescription. To avoid a call from your patient (or maybe from her lawyer), it makes sense to provide counseling on your antibiotic choice. Since there are alternatives to use of nitrofurantoins and sulfa/trimethoprim in the first trimester, it is wise to do so even if the evidence is limited. Avoid sulfonamides in the third trimester to avoid the known association with hyperbilirubinemia [high blood levels of bilirubin].

A more important consideration is the reproductive age non-pregnant patient that presents or calls with UTI symptoms. Is it safe to use nitrofurantoin or sulfa drugs in these women? In contrast to the patient at 8 weeks, these are exactly the individuals in whom an early fetal exposure is possible. Consider carefully the drug resistance patterns in your community, and the contraceptive status of your patient when considering therapy. If she is at high risk for pregnancy, best to avoid these drugs.

Reference

Crider KS, et al. Antibacterial medication during pregnancy and risk of birth defects: National Birth Defects Prevention Study. *Arch Pediatr Adolesc Med* 2009;163:978–985.

Periodical and Internet Sources Bibliography

The following articles have been selected to supplement the diverse views presented in this chapter.

Gavin Aronsen	"Fewer Mountaintops, More Birth Defects," *Mother Jones*, June 22, 2011.
José Bellver, Marco Melo, and Sergio R. Soares	"The Impact of Cigarette Smoking on the Health of Descendants," *Expert Review of Obstetrics and Gynecology*, March 2012.
Christina Chambers	"Drugs, Pregnancy, and Lactation: Antibacterial Use in Pregnancy," *OB GYN News*, August 2011.
Christina Chambers	"NSAIDS in the First Trimester," *Family Practice News*, September 15, 2012.
Tracy Clark-Flory	"Russian Roulette with Birth Defect Meds," *Salon*, October 23, 2010. www.salon.com.
James Fallows	"China's Pollution: The Birth Defect Angle," *Atlantic Monthly*, January 29, 2013.
Allan Hackshaw, Charles Rodeck, and Sadie Boniface	"Maternal Smoking in Pregnancy and Birth Defects: A Systematic Review Based on 173,687 Malformed Cases and 11.7 Million Controls," *Human Reproduction Update*, July 11, 2011.
Gideon Koren	"Opioids and Birth Defects," *OB GYN News*, July 2011.
Claire Perlman	"Herbicide Associated with Birth Defects in Infants," *Earth Island Journal*, June 29, 2011.
Jonathan Stone and Roger Williams	"The Nazis at the Heart of the Worst Drug Scandal of All Time," *Newsweek*, September 17, 2012.

CHAPTER 3

Should Pregnant Women Undergo Screening for Birth Defects?

Chapter Preface

Not all birth defects can be detected with prenatal screening tests; however, for certain common defects, there are tests that can detect—with varying degrees of accuracy—the presence of a congenital abnormality. Some of the birth defects for which there are screening tests include: neural tube defects, such as spina bifida; abdominal wall defects, such as gastroschisis; heart defects; and chromosomal defects, such as Down syndrome. The reasons for screening vary, and the question of what should be done with such information has created controversy about the screening itself, especially since screening has become less risky and more informative.

Screening for birth defects can occur prior to conception with carrier testing. Carrier testing, or screening, is a type of genetic testing of prospective parents to see whether they are carriers for genes that could result in birth defects. For certain people with a high risk of being carriers for a certain disease, carrier screening may be advised. Cystic fibrosis, for instance, is a hereditary condition that results in the overproduction of mucus, leading to damage to several organs of the body and shortened lifespan. For a couple where each has a relative with cystic fibrosis, carrier screening could determine whether they are both carriers, having one copy of the genetic mutation. If a male carrier and a female carrier have a child together, the child will have cystic fibrosis. Thus, carrier screening can help a couple determine their risk for having a child with a particular birth defect, allowing them to choose to forgo pregnancy or to engage in further screening if they do become pregnant.

After conception, there are a variety of tests available to pregnant women, including ultrasound exams, blood tests, amniocentesis, and chorionic villus sampling (CVS). Ultrasound exams are frequently performed during the first trimester of pregnancy and can assess the risk of birth defects such as Down syndrome and heart abnormalities. Blood tests can be used on their own or in conjunction with other screenings to assess the risk of birth defects. In the second trimester, multiple marker screening tests for three or four substances in the blood that could indicate Down syndrome and neural tube defects. Ultrasound screening and blood tests are quite routine and are safe for the pregnant woman and the fetus, but even together are unable to give a definitive diagnosis of any particular birth defect: Certainty through combined screening can reach 90 to 95 percent for a birth defect such as Down syndrome, although not until the second trimester, fifteen to twenty weeks into pregnancy.

If abnormalities are suspected, the woman may decide to undergo riskier screening, such as amniocentesis, where amniotic fluid and cells are taken from the sac surrounding the fetus, or CVS, where cells from the placenta are tested. Both of these procedures risk causing a miscarriage but offer a more definitive diagnosis, so the decision to undergo them is one that must be weighed by the pregnant woman and her doctor.

The recent availability of cell-free fetal DNA tests is rapidly altering the field of prenatal screening. Since 2011, the tests have been gaining acceptance by doctors and insurance companies and offer pregnant women the ability to test for certain birth defects such as Down syndrome as early as ten weeks into pregnancy with an alleged certainty rate approaching 100 percent.

Knowing of birth defects during pregnancy can allow prospective parents to decide whether to continue with pregnancy, but it also can allow them to prepare for a child with special needs or prepare for or even begin treatment of certain conditions. As the viewpoints in this chapter illustrate, it is the option to terminate that is often fraught with controversy. Yet, as genetic testing advances, there are also issues about the relevance of having more information. The question of whether pregnant women should undergo prenatal screening has never been more timely, as the advent of more and more tests will also raise the question of whether there is such a thing as too much information.

| *"Without comprehensive prenatal ultra-sound, women are at the mercy of conventional 'risk-based' screening."*

Routine Prenatal Screening Should Be Available to Pregnant Women

Darshak Sanghavi

In the following viewpoint, Darshak Sanghavi argues that the kind of information available to pregnant women through prenatal screening is important because it allows the treatment of birth defects in many cases and gives women the opportunity to terminate the pregnancy or prepare for babies with birth defects. Sanghavi claims that complete fetal ultrasounds should be available to pregnant women, along with counseling. Sanghavi is chief of pediatric cardiology and an associate professor of pediatrics at the University of Massachusetts Medical School, as well as the health care columnist for Slate *magazine.*

As you read, consider the following questions:

1. What percentage of American pregnancies, according to Sanghavi, are complicated by either serious birth defects or chromosomal defects?

2. According to the author, what fraction of babies with missing limbs are not known to be missing limbs until birth?

3. According to Sanghavi, which two countries have the highest detection rates for major birth defects?

Here's something to freak out expectant parents: Over 2 percent of all American pregnancies are complicated by serious birth defects, and more than 0.5 percent of all fetuses have either a missing or an extra chromosome—a condition that leads to problems like Down or Edwards syndrome. Birth defects are a leading cause of infant mortality in the country, and most problems occur in pregnancies without any obvious risk factors. (For example, most babies with Down syndrome are born to women under 35 years of age.) There are ways to screen fetuses for birth defects like these, but due to a lack of clear guidance from caregivers or policymakers, parents may not find out about them until it's too late.

The Importance of Knowledge

Knowing about problems before birth is important for at least two reasons. First, it allows doctors to treat the condition. Take heart problems, where a major artery may be connected incorrectly or a pumping chamber may be missing. Prenatal detection and immediate treatment at birth can prevent the sudden oxygen deprivation and shock that might occur if doctors were surprised by the defect. Some types of spina bifida can be surgically fixed before birth, preventing future paralysis.

A second benefit of prenatal screening is that it gives families a chance to decide whether they wish to continue a pregnancy at all. A huge number of women now choose abortion when faced with major birth defects. In Hawaii, which collects comprehensive information on pregnancy outcomes, more than 90 percent of women who learn they have a fetus with Down syndrome choose to terminate their pregnancies. (Other states are likely to have similar proportions.) Roughly one-half of all women whose babies have brain defects or major abdominal defects also elect abortion. To be sure, many families continue their pregnancies, and love and nurture their babies. Such families deserve support from doctors and insurers. But many families choose differently and they also deserve support.

Most of the time, however, expectant parents never realize there might be a problem. Major heart defects go unnoticed until birth an astounding 70 percent of the time. Three-quarters of all babies with missing limbs come as a surprise to both doctors and patients. More than one-half of cases of Down syndrome are overlooked. The list goes on and on.

The Outdated RADIUS Study

Why are we missing so many important birth defects during pregnancy? Insurers and advisory groups don't support the necessary procedures. To diagnose the vast majority of problems—such as those related to the heart, lung, gut, and brain—one must visualize the fetus's body by ultrasound during the second trimester. But back in 1993, the *New England Journal of Medicine* reported results from the so-called RADIUS study (that's "Routine Antenatal Diagnostic Imaging with Ultrasound"). According to its findings, the blanket use of such ultrasounds "clearly indicate" no impact on a baby's outcome; parents would do just as well by letting their doctors decide whether to do the scans on a case-by-case basis. As a result, several insurance companies, such as Aetna, don't cover comprehensive fetal scans for routine pregnancies—a policy that affects roughly one-third of American women. The American Congress of Obstetricians and Gynecologists does not recommend the scan for all women, either. (When my wife was pregnant with our first child, our obstetrician actually advised us to make up a family history of birth defects, since our insurer wouldn't cover the scan in a normal pregnancy.)

Yet the RADIUS study, now almost 20 years old, shouldn't guide our approach today. First, treatments have gotten better. RADIUS actually showed that screening increased the number of major birth defects identified by a factor of more than 3—but given the therapies for heart defects and other problems that were available back then, this extra information didn't help. Second, the technology for scanning fetuses has vastly improved. At least one-half of the detections of major birth defects in the RADIUS study came too late for women to consider pregnancy termination; if we did the study over using today's technology, it's very likely that would change. Third, many parents want to know whether their unborn child has a major birth defect, even if there's nothing they can do about it. (As with many screening tests, false positives worry doctors and policymakers. However, even the RADIUS study showed no measurable harms to babies from ultrasound screening.)

At this point, almost every obstetrician in the country who manages high-risk pregnancies thinks ultrasound screenings are a good idea—so long as they they're done in a high-quality, high-volume center. (A good center is key since the doctors' and technicians' skills vary a lot. Just this month [October 2011], I saw a pregnant patient who'd been assured her baby was fine, yet a week before birth our ultrasound detected clear signs of a major heart defect, missing stomach, and a malformed brain, among other problems.) Among large, developed Western nations, only the United States, the Netherlands, and Spain fail to recommend complete fetal ultrasounds for all pregnant women. (Germany and France, which have the highest detection rates for major defects, recommend a complete scan every trimester.)

The Need for Professional Advice

Without comprehensive prenatal ultrasound, women are at the mercy of conventional "risk-based" screening, in the form of a blood test that provides information on three (and only three) potential problems: spina bifida, Down syndrome, and Edwards syndrome. By measuring the levels of estriol, alpha-fetoprotein, and several other substances in a pregnant woman, the test assigns a certain *probability* to each defect. The lab report reads like a Vegas betting line. For example, a woman of a given age might have a baseline 1-in-476 chance of having a baby with Down syndrome before she even takes the test, and then be told that her true risk, determined from her blood sample, is 1 in 51. (In 2007, ACOG [American Congress of Obstetricians and Gynecologists] added an ultrasound measurement of the fetus's neck to the standard test, but continued the practice of reporting proportions.)

That's a problem because many patients find these statistics utterly baffling. In 1999, researchers found that one-half of all patients can't make sense of them; for example, many think a 1-in-200 risk of a birth defect is more favorable than a 1-in-400. Perhaps as a result, few women with elevated risks choose to have amniocentesis, the follow-up procedure that would give a more definitive result.

Amniocentesis carries its own risks: It causes miscarriages at a rate that falls between 1 in 300 and 1 in 1,600. How should one probability be weighed against another? Many patients aren't sure. Interestingly, no regulatory authority tracks doctors' complication rates with amniocentesis, and ACOG does not set a minimum number of procedures for each doctor per year (meaning that your doctor may not do them often enough to stay sharp).

National Policy/Recommendations for Routine Prenatal Ultrasound Scans in Place in 2004 in Eighteen European Countries

Countries	Routine ultrasound scan policy/ recommendations	Gestation at routine scans (weeks)
Austria	Two scans	10–14*, 18–22, 30–44
Belgium	Three scans	10–14, 18–23, 29–33
Croatia	One scan	10–14*, 18–23, 34–37*
Denmark	Two scans	10–14 (nuchal), 18
England and Wales	Two scans	10–12, 18–23
Finland	One or two scans	16–19 if only one scan, 13–14 and 18–20 if two scans
France	Three scans	10–14, 18–23, 29–32
Germany	Three scans	9–12, 19–22, 29–32
Ireland	No national policy	18–22*
Italy	Three scans	10–14, 18–23, 30
Malta	No national policy	18–23*, 34–25*
Netherlands	No national policy	No routine scans
Norway	One scan	18
Portugal	Three scans	10–14, 18–23, 29–33
Poland	Three scans	11–14, 18–22, 28–32
Spain	No national policy– practice varies between regions	10–14*, 18–23*, 29–33*
Sweden	Two scans	10–14, 16–17
Switzerland	Two scans	11–14, 20–22

*Not official policy but usually performed.

TAKEN FROM: PA Boyd, et al., "Survey of Prenatal Screening Policies in Europe for Structural Malformations and Chromosomal Anomalies, and Their Impact on Detection and Termination Rates for Neural Tube Defects and Down's Syndrome," *BJOG: An International Journal of Obstetrics and Gynecology*, vol. 115. no. 6, May 2008.

Given all these concerns, what should expectant women do? No test can catch every problem, of course. Here's the bottom line: Until sophisticated new blood tests or high-quality scans become widely available—for example, one that provides the same information as amniocentesis but without the risks of miscarriage—the best resource to help navigate prenatal testing is a genetics counselor. These professionals, typically on staff at large birth centers, help women make sense of their options for prenatal testing—and remind them that the usual blood tests cover only a few, relatively uncommon problems. (They also may guide couples of certain high-risk populations, like Ashkenazi Jews, to more specialized testing.) For now, women should also consider a comprehensive fetal ultrasound in the second trimester at a high-volume, tertiary-care center. Otherwise, they may be turning a blind eye to their baby's health.

> *"The cell-free fetal DNA test gives expectant mothers an earlier (and safer) look than ever at [their unborn babies]."*

New Prenatal Genetic Tests Offer Safe Early Screening for Birth Defects

Erin Biba

In the following viewpoint, Erin Biba argues that a new blood test available to pregnant women in early pregnancy allows the safe detection of birth defects earlier than ever. She claims that the test will now detect chromosomal abnormalities but in the future will give much more information, allowing pregnant women the ability to terminate a pregnancy earlier or have more information in preparation for the birth of a child. Biba is a science and technology reporter and writer.

As you read, consider the following questions:

1. When did the new prenatal blood test come on the market, according to Biba?

2. According to the author, what is the problem with older blood tests that measure hormones and proteins in a pregnant woman's bloodstream?

3. According to Biba, the American Congress of Obstetricians and Gynecologists made what recommendations regarding the new cell-free fetal DNA test?

Candace Weiss didn't know she had a family history of birth defects until she got pregnant with her daughter. That's when she learned that her grandmother, at the age of 42, had given birth to a baby with Down syndrome. "That child died young," she says. "But back in that time, they sent them away. She wasn't even raised in the family."

Weiss' own child was born perfectly healthy. Not long after, she and her husband started trying for a second baby. But she had a miscarriage. And then another. The second miscarriage was the result of triploid syndrome—the fetus had three of every chromosome instead of the normal two. So when Weiss, a 32-year-old lawyer turned stay-at-home mom in Westchester, New York (her name has been changed for this story), got pregnant again, her doctors watched her closely. "We did a lot of ultrasounds," she says. "Everything looked like it was going well."

A New Blood Test

Many women with high-risk pregnancies (which also includes women over 35) elect to undergo amniocentesis or chorionic villus samplings—invasive procedures that check for chromosomal abnormalities but carry with them a risk of miscarriage. Weiss says there was "no way in hell" she was going to do that. She didn't want to risk losing another baby. Well, said her doctor at her 10-week office visit, we've got this new test that checks for the most common chromosomal disorders (like Down syndrome). All it requires is a blood draw. And you can do it right now. The test was so new, in fact, that Weiss was one of the first patients in her doctor's practice to have it.

A week or so later the doctor called. The baby had Down syndrome. "We were obviously shocked," Weiss says. "Even the doctor was shocked." Weiss then had a chorionic villus sampling performed, on the remote chance of a false positive. It confirmed the blood test result, but she and her husband were already resigned to what was to follow. She says she needed to talk through the decision to end the pregnancy, but her husband never had any doubt. "His coping mechanism was just to be done with it," Weiss says. But for her, it was a bit different. "You hear this news and you make your decision. But meanwhile you're still pregnant. I mean, I was still nauseous."

Weiss terminated the pregnancy last fall at 12 and a half weeks. She and her husband hadn't told very many people that she was pregnant, and the procedure at that stage is mercifully swift and relatively simple. Some women do not find out their babies have serious medical problems until much later in their pregnancies. At that point, many doctors don't even perform abortions, obliging patients to travel to distant cities to get one. "It's huge to know early on," Weiss says. "Not that what we went through wasn't heartbreaking, but we were able to put it behind us faster. We get to start over sooner."

The Risks of Prenatal Testing

Before she knew about the blood test, Weiss—like hundreds of thousands of pregnant women each year—had been facing a complicated decision: Risk a perfectly healthy pregnancy to find out for sure if there's something wrong with your child, or live with a degree of uncertainty. It's a trade-off inherent in prenatal tests. Some are accurate—they can say for sure whether a child has a serious disorder—but may cause side effects; others are safer but give a more ambiguous level of information—all you get is the odds of whether or not the child has problems.

Yet plenty of patients today still go ahead with risky prenatal tests anyway. About 200,000 amniocenteses are performed in the US every year; the miscarriage rate for those is between 1 in 400 and 1 in 200. The miscarriage rate for chorionic villus sampling (CVS) is between 1 in 200 and 1 in 100, and it carries other risks, including infection and, in very rare cases, birth defects.

But with the advent of the kind of test Weiss took, which first hit the market in October 2011, there's an option that's about as accurate as amnio and CVS but as low-risk as a blood draw. Known as cell-free fetal DNA testing, it's now offered by Sequenom, Verinata, and Ariosa Diagnostics. The new test is expected to upend how prenatal screening and diagnosis are done—as well as create a financial windfall for the labs that perform it. (Market research firm Frost & Sullivan estimates that revenue in the prenatal testing industry will grow to $1.6 billion by 2017, up from $1.3 billion in 2010.) For the most part, the tests offered by these companies check for only three of the most common chromosomal disorders, but that's just the beginning. They presage a future when we can easily scan for a range of genetic defects, from the truly devastating to the not-so-serious, allowing parents and doctors to look past a baby's organs, beyond its cells, and down into its very DNA. Based on a small sample of a woman's blood, the cell-free fetal DNA test gives expectant mothers an earlier (and safer) look than ever at just who it is that's growing inside them.

The History of Prenatal Tests

The first time anyone got a peek into the womb was in 1896. X-rays had recently been discovered, and Edward Parker Davis, professor of obstetrics at Jefferson Medical College in Philadelphia, decided to use the new technology to observe a fetus inside a pregnant woman. Easily able to see the skull of the baby on the photographic plate, Davis later wrote in his *Manual of Obstetrics*: "When pregnancy is advanced so far that the fetal skeleton is well formed, the x-ray will give an outline of the fetus which may be available for diagnosis . . . The position of the child in the pelvis, the presence of pelvic deformity, multiple pregnancy, and sometimes fetal deformity maybe outlined in this way."

It was, quite literally, a revelation. Before long, doctors started to use x-rays on pregnant women regularly. And, despite the fact that early radiological technology was so primitive that the patient had to sit still for up to an hour with her feet on a stool, arching over the back of a chair and thrusting her belly toward the machine, the practice began to catch on.

At first, doctors used the procedure to determine, say, if a woman was carrying twins. Then, in 1916, surgeon James Thomas Case was working with a patient who at seven months pregnant could no longer feel her baby moving. Case turned to the x-ray. He discovered that the baby was missing its cranial bones—the fetus had not developed a large part of its brain and skull. Ultimately Case induced labor, and the baby was stillborn. But with this first-ever diagnosis of a fetal abnormality, he proved that the x-ray could be a powerful tool for prenatal medicine; even though evidence emerged in the 1950s suggesting that radiation was a danger to fetuses, it would continue to be used into the 1980s.

By then, other prenatal tests had come along. But you always had to choose. Safe? Or accurate? Amniocentesis, for example, involves doctors inserting a long needle through the mother's abdomen and into the uterus to sample the fluid bath that envelops the growing fetus. The procedure provides clear data about some potential birth defects—technicians essentially examine chromosomes under a microscope—but the risk of miscarriage has persisted since the technique was developed in the 1960s. The accurate CVS test, which gained popularity in the 1980s, can be done earlier, but because it too involves a long needle or tube (either through the abdomen or cervix) it exposes the fetus to risks. Blood tests called multiple marker screens, meanwhile, measure specific hormones and proteins in the mother's bloodstream. Abnormal levels raise red flags and indicate that a more invasive and definitive test—amniocentesis or CVS—should be performed. Unfortunately, these blood tests produce numerous false negatives and false positives. So some serious problems are missed altogether and some tests result in unnecessary procedures, which, in turn, cause an estimated 1,000 miscarriages of healthy fetuses every year.

The Cell-Free Fetal DNA Test

The cell-free fetal DNA test totally upends this equation. And it relies on the slightly creepy fact that the bloodstream of a pregnant woman is full of genetic material from her baby. Some of this DNA is inside the nucleus of intact fetal cells, and some is just floating around loose. We've known about the intact cells since the 1970s. As a fetus develops, the placenta sheds some of its cells. And each of them contains a set of the baby's chromosomes—the 23 pairs of curled-up packets that house a human's genetic material. Some of those intact cells (plus a few other types, like red and white blood cells) migrate into the mother's bloodstream with the baby's DNA on board. The problem, from a prenatal testing point of view, is that these cells are extremely rare and difficult to isolate from a sea of maternal blood. Plus, they can remain present for years. This means that you would only get useful test readings during a woman's first pregnancy.

But fetal DNA gets into the mother's bloodstream another way too: As cells from the placenta die and come apart, the loose "cell-free" genetic material they carry seeps into the mother's system. In fact, around 10 percent of all the free-floating DNA in a pregnant woman's blood plasma belongs to her baby. About a day after the mother gives birth, this genetic evidence disappear—it's filtered out by the kidneys—leaving a clean slate for testing subsequent pregnancies.

Cell-free fetal DNA was discovered about 15 years ago by a scientist named Dennis Lo. He had come across two papers

Comparing the Old and New Blood Tests

	Multiple-Marker Screening Test	Cell-Free Fetal DNA Test
Number screening	100,000	100,000
Down syndrome prevalence	1 in 500 (N=200)	1 in 500 (N=200)
Detection rate (%)	80	99
False positive rate (%)	5	0.2
Down syndrome fetuses identified (N)	160 (out of 200)	198 (out of 200)
False-positive results (N)	4,990 (out of 99,880)	200 (out of 99,800)
Positive predictive value (%)	3.1	49.7
Odd of having an affected fetus	1 to 31	1 to 1

TAKEN FROM: David Grenache, "Should DNA-Based Test for Down Syndrome Screening Replace Biochemical Tests?" *Pregnancy Lab* (blog), January 6, 2013. www.pregnancylab.net.

in *Nature Medicine* describing free-floating tumor DNA in the blood plasma of cancer patients. "I thought that if a tumor could release sufficient DNA into the circulation for us to detect it, then surely we should be able to find fetal DNA in the plasma of pregnant women," he says. The notion would ultimately make Lo famous in the world of obstetrics and prenatal testing. He's now director of the Li Ka Shing Institute of Health Sciences in Hong Kong and a member of Sequenom's clinical advisory board.

Starting in 1996, Lo's research team began searching for the Y chromosome of male fetuses in the blood plasma of pregnant women (since only boys have Y chromosomes, if they were found in a woman's bloodstream, they'd have to belong to the baby). They guessed that a baby's DNA would be relatively easy to find in the later stages of pregnancy—after all, the larger the baby grew the more DNA it would release, right? What they discovered, however, was that they could detect fetal DNA as early as six weeks (although testing at about 10 weeks yields more accurate results because DNA levels are higher). The implications were enormous. Getting a sample was easy, and it could be done much earlier than amniocentesis (usually performed between the 16th and 18th weeks of pregnancy) and even a bit earlier than CVS (often done in the 12-week range). If the results meant that the parents chose an abortion, the timing at least would be a little easier on the family. If the test was normal, as it usually would be, the parents could breathe a sigh of relief that much earlier. "The scientific community has been looking for a noninvasive way to perform prenatal diagnostics for the past 20 years," says Dirk van den Boom, Sequenom's senior vice president of research and development. "You take away a lot of anxiety when you get accurate results early in the pregnancy."

The Detection of Chromosomal Abnormalities

Sequenom, the first company to offer this test, is located just down the road from the beautiful oceanfront scenery of the Scripps Institution of Oceanography in La Jolla, California. Its dull office-park headquarters is about what you'd expect for a blood-test operation: Every day, boxes filled with samples arrive from doctors' offices around the country. The tubes of blood are unpacked and stored in a freezer at -80 degrees Fahrenheit. When it's time to test, they're placed into centrifuges and the plasma is separated out. But appearances can be deceiving. In the next room over sit millions of dollars' worth of next-generation genetic sequencers. It may look dull, but this was the first testing lab in the US to use sequencers in a large-scale, high-throughput prenatal test.

Green lights on the boxy sequencers hum back and forth, making them look a little like Cylons [cyborgs in the old TV series *Battlestar Gallactica*]. The machines are searching for chromosomal abnormalities called trisomies. That's a genetic defect where, instead of having the usual two copies of a particular chromosome in each cell, the fetus has three. Most newborns affected by this have problems with chromosomes 13, 18, and 21, and the sex chromosomes (X and Y). Trisomy 21, better known as Down syndrome (after John Langdon Down, who first described it in 1866), is characterized by physical features like upward slanting eyes and a flattened nose. People with the disorder can live into adulthood, but they experience a range of mild to severe mental disabilities, heart defects, hearing problems, and difficulty seeing. The prospects for self-sufficient living in adulthood vary depending on the severity. Many are able to care for themselves, but those with severe disabilities require assistance throughout their lives.

The effects of a triple-set of the 18th chromosome (known as Edwards syndrome) and of the 13th (known as Patau syndrome) are far more serious. Many children born with these disorders live only a few days, and 90 percent die before their first birthday (though there are outliers—2012 Republican presidential hopeful Rick Santorum has a daughter with Edwards syndrome who is almost 5 years old). In fact, many affected fetuses naturally miscarry—though this can happen painfully late in a pregnancy. As a woman gets older, her likelihood of having a child with one of these conditions increases: At 25, her chances of giving birth to a child with Down are 1 in 1,250. By age 35—not an uncommon age for women to have a child these days—they jump to 1 in 378. In 2007 the increasing accuracy of screening meant that the American Congress of Obstetricians and Gynecologists decided to throw out old guidelines that recommended screening only for pregnant women over 35 and instead advised offering it to all women, regardless of age. Because of the chance of side effects, however, patients usually opt for invasive testing only if they are high-risk or if there is an indication that something may be wrong with the pregnancy. Up to 85 percent of parents in the US who discover their child has Down syndrome opt for abortion.

To detect chromosomal abnormalities, Sequenom uses a technique called massively parallel shotgun sequencing. (Companies could also take a more targeted approach that analyzes only the relevant chromosomes.) First they use PCR technology to make copies of millions of snippets of DNA in the blood sample, then they sift through the mix for specific sections that scientists know show up only on, say, chromosome 21. Think of it as a bowl of M&Ms, where the brown ones represent segments of chromosome 21. You expect to find a factory-set proportion of them, and you know that some come from the mom and some from the baby. If the fetus has three copies of chromosome 21 instead of the normal two, you're going to find too many brown M&Ms in your bowl. This means there's a problem.

New Prenatal Testing Recommendations

At the end of November [2012], the American Congress of Obstetricians and Gynecologists released a long-awaited opinion on the cell-free fetal DNA test. The group recommended it for patients at an increased risk for chromosomal defects, including those over age 35 and those with a history of trisomy pregancies. It did not advise using the test as a routine part of prenatal care for low-risk patients or women who are carrying multiples. The recommendation is likely to make doctors more aware of the test; many ob-gyns [obstetrics-gynecology physicians] have never even heard of it, and though some insurance companies have worked out coverage for the test, many patients are paying around $500 out of pocket.

Until news of the test reaches more physicians, demand will largely be driven by the women themselves, many of whom find out about it online. Jennifer Schaefer, a 38-year-old Google employee and mother of two, first heard about the test on parenting message boards. Her ob-gyn didn't know about it, so Schaefer requested the test from her genetic counselor. She isn't so unusual. Very often, women who hear about the new blood test immediately seek it out. (One doctor points out that her more educated, higher-socioeconomic-status patients are the ones who ask for it the most.) Indeed, Sequenom alone has run 37,000 tests since its version debuted in October 2011. That said, most women still end up having an ultrasound, a noninvasive peek at the developing baby that can tell doctors about other issues like neural tube defects or, later in pregnancy, kidney or heart problems.

Interestingly, it's not at all clear that the cell-free fetal DNA test will increase abortion rates. Some 90 percent of all genetically disabled babies are already identified in utero—further detection would add only that last 10 percent. "I wouldn't think there's going to be a dramatic increase" in abortion if the new test proliferates, says Joanne Taylor, a genetic-counseling supervisor at Lucile Packard Children's Hospital in Palo Alto, California. "You're only adding babies that wouldn't have been seen before—say, in a 22-year-old woman who wouldn't have been screened in the past. They'll be added to the pool to make a decision. You're looking at a small group to begin with."

And some families, of course, choose to continue with the pregnancy. They, too, could take advantage of this test: Studies have shown that when it comes to Down syndrome, the psychological benefits of early knowledge are significant. "Most families report that they are happy to have learned the information during the pregnancy," Taylor says. "They can prepare and not have a shock at delivery that they have to quickly adjust to."

The Future of Prenatal Testing

The cell-free fetal DNA test will eventually be able to look for more than just the big three chromosomal disorders. In fact, Verinata just announced that it will offer a screen for Turner and Klinefelter syndromes along with other sex chromosome disorders. Turner syndrome affects about one in 2,000 births, and it results when one of a girl's two X chromosomes is missing or incomplete. Cases can be quite mild, but women with Turner can exhibit a webbed neck, infertility, and heart problems. Klinefelter affects about 1 in 1,000 boys—they have two X chromosomes and a Y instead of the normal XY pair. Boys with Klinefelter might have the suggestion of breasts, less body hair, impaired fertility, and a higher propensity for other diseases, but they can and do lead pretty normal lives. A cheap, easy, safe test for conditions like these raises uncomfortable questions: Your slightly soft-bodied high school math teacher could well have had Klinefelter syndrome, maybe without even knowing it. This makes the decision to abort a baby with Klinefelter a lot more difficult than the decision to abort a trisomy 18 pregnancy.

Other, further-out applications of this test might include looking for issues like Tay-Sachs (usually fatal), sickle cell anemia and cystic fibrosis (both survivable with treatment), or even the presence of the BRCA1 or BRCA2 gene, which are associated with a high likelihood of some breast cancers. But as Glenn Palomaki, associate director of the Institute for Preventive Medicine and Medical Screening and head of the independent research team that validated Sequenom's test, puts it, "If you can test for 20 disorders, should you do 40? 60? 400?"

John Stuelpnagel, executive chair at Ariosa Diagnostics, which offers a cell-free fetal DNA test, says the way to think about future options is like this: You want to test for things that are either really severe and have a clear-cut diagnosis, or you want to test for milder conditions that can be treated in some way. "The genetic disorder must be well understood," he says. "It does not benefit anyone if there is ambiguity in diagnosis created by a test."

For now, then, and into the foreseeable future, we'll have to be content with accepting that humans exist on a kind of bell curve of normalcy: No matter how deep we poke and prod and look and worry, our ability—and our desire—to know who our children are before they are born will always have limits. Until they come squalling into the world, there's not much more to do but watch and wait. Which makes us little different than those mothers in the late 1800s, backs bent over chairs, bellies thrust into the air, hoping for the best.

| "[Fetal genome testing entails] ethically
  and legally sensitive issues."

New Prenatal Genetic Tests Raise Tricky Ethical Questions

Harriet A. Washington

In the following viewpoint, Harriet A. Washington argues that new genetics tests currently in development will offer vast amounts of genetic information, but she worries that more information is not necessarily a good thing. Washington contends that such information may cause anxiety, could be useless, and will lead to a host of sensitive situations regarding what to do with the information. Washington is author of Deadly Monopolies: The Shocking Corporate Takeover of Life Itself—and the Consequences for Your Health and Our Medical Future.

As you read, consider the following questions:

1. The new genetic tests that Washington discusses both rely on what fact about fetal DNA?

2. Washington claims that what percentage of women who currently have prenatal tests receive bad news?

3. What birth defect does the author cite as evidence of how changing perceptions of disorders can change the experience of having such disorders?

Boy or girl? This you can easily discover, but wouldn't you like to know more? If you could peer into your baby's medical future, what traits would you most want assurance about?

Most parents wouldn't hesitate: a healthy child. Soon science will be able to help them with that more quickly, completely—and safely—than ever before.

Two New Prenatal Tests

In June [2012], a team at the University of Washington in Seattle announced a new technique that enables the construction of a comprehensive genome sequence—a genetic "blueprint", as they described it—of the developing fetus from as early as the first trimester. The test could be available in clinics in as little as five years [dating from 2012].

Then, in July, a team at Stanford University in California announced a slightly different technique for obtaining the same information.

Both techniques rely on the fact that fetal DNA circulates in the mother's bloodstream and can be isolated and sequenced. The Seattle test needs only a sample of saliva or blood from the father and blood from the mother. After determining the parents' genomes, it is possible to discern which DNA comes from the fetus. The Stanford test requires only maternal blood.

Both tests are non-invasive, thus avoiding the 2 per cent risk of miscarriage posed by today's most common antenatal genetic tests, amniocentesis and chorionic villus sampling. These require a needle to be inserted into the amniotic sac so that the fetal DNA can be tested for Down's syndrome and other genetic disorders.

The existing antenatal tests can also spot other chromosomal abnormalities, including cystic fibrosis, trisomy 13, and Turner, Klinefelter and fragile-X syndromes. In contrast, the genetic blueprint can finger thousands of potentially problematic genes. It is "like going from being able to see that two books are stuck together to being able to notice one word misspelled on a page", says Jacob Kitzman, a member of the University of Washington team.

The benefit is a medical early warning on a previously unknown scale. Children with the genetic disorder phenylketonuria, for example, are usually diagnosed after birth and must be put on a strict, lifelong diet. Knowing the child's status beforehand would be helpful.

The Price of Genetic Knowledge

Given this and other potential benefits, should we not hasten to make blueprint screening mandatory, as many newborn tests are today? Not until we know more, and maybe not even then.

Today, only around 5 per cent of women who have prenatal tests receive bad news. Full genome screens will detect many more problems—and will introduce much more uncertainty because whole-genome mapping predicts the mere possibility of disease. Not all genetic anomalies are expressed as pathology.

The test will also produce false positives that frighten parents into thinking their child will have a disability when in fact he or she will be healthy.

For that matter, what is "healthy" anyway? When is a genetic anomaly a disease? Males with the chromosome disorder XYY were once thought to have a high risk of violent behaviour, and many XYY fetuses were aborted. But research has shown that XYY males are essentially normal.

The price of genetic knowledge can be high because of the anxiety caused by the knowledge of a propensity for a disease that has no known treatment or cure, or that may never appear.

The Usefulness of More Information

Before using such a test, parents must ask themselves "what can we do with the information?" If abortion is not an option, perhaps because the fetus is past the maximum gestation period or because of moral beliefs, the information can be useless—or worse than useless, thanks to the needless anxiety. Moreover, the dearth of treatment options for some disorders makes the information medically useless, but potentially risky if insurers use it to hike rates or deny cover.

If abortion is an option, new problems emerge: which disorders justify abortion? For some conditions the choice is perhaps clearer. For example, children with the infantile form of Tay-Sachs or Canavan disease go into an immediate, inexorable decline. There is no cure or effective treatment and most children with the disease die in childhood.

But what of genes that entail a higher risk of Alzheimer's, typical prostate cancers or Huntington's [an incurable neurodegenerative disorder]? These diseases emerge only after decades of productive life, and may not emerge at all.

Changing perceptions of disorders over time must also be taken into consideration. For example, we have seen a cultural sea change in the perception of Down's syndrome. Fifty years ago, parents were often advised to institutionalise affected children. Today people with the condition mostly live in mainstream society and have found wide acceptance.

Other Ethical Issues

There are other ethically and legally sensitive issues. Who has a right to a child's genetic information? If the screen reveals an unmanageable condition such as Huntington's that will not

New Genetic Testing and Minor Birth Defects

Future applications of NIPD [non-invasive prenatal genetic diagnosis] may be used to detect and select against pregnancies with such seemingly minor genetic conditions as a missing finger (ectrodactyly). Recall the controversial account of [California news anchor] Bree Walker Lampley, whose decision to have children carrying her genetic trait for ectrodactyly (a genetic condition causing a deletion in the digits of the hands and feet) caused public backlash. Radio talk-show host Jane Norris spent two hours of her show questioning whether it was *fair* of Lampley to risk having more "deformed" children, and taking calls from listeners who suggested it was "irresponsible" to bear a child with such traits. The impact that NIPD will have on the already contentious issues regarding "minor" disabling conditions is difficult to determine. What can be said is that NIPD will allow for faster, and perhaps rash, decisions about all fetal characteristics that may diverge from the "norm."

Lori Haymon,
Council for Responsible Genetics, 2011.

manifest until the child is old enough to make his or her own decisions, should the parents decide whether to share the information with other family members who may share the risk? Should there be regulations that compel a physician or the parents to alert siblings and others who may be at high risk of harbouring the gene?

The Seattle test can also reveal unexpected paternity. Should doctors have to disclose this, or should parents be able to opt out of being informed?

Whole-genome fetal sequencing is still years away from being used in the real world. It's a good [thing], as we have a lot to sort out before then.

> "Who among us exhibit a greater un-
> conditional love capacity than our
> brothers and sisters with Down syn-
> drome? To the extent that they and
> other 'defectives' are unwelcome among
> us can be measured our own deficien-
> cies as a society."

Love Is the Antidote to Prenatal Eugenic Cleansing

Wesley J. Smith

In the following viewpoint, Wesley J. Smith argues that prenatal testing is being used for a kind of eugenic cleansing where most fetuses with imperfections are aborted. Smith claims that if unconditional love were a stronger cultural norm, then prenatal testing could be used to inform parents rather than to eliminate imperfections. Smith's blog, Human Exceptionalism, *is hosted by* National Review Online, *and he is a senior fellow at the Discovery Institute's Center on Human Exceptionalism, as well as the author of* Culture of Death: The Assault on Medical Ethics in America.

As you read, consider the following questions:

1. According to the author, what percentage of fetuses with Down syndrome and dwarfism are aborted?

2. An Oregon couple was awarded $2.9 million for what reason, according to Smith?

3. The author suggests that if the current prenatal testing technology had existed earlier, Abraham Lincoln might have been aborted for what reason?

Scientists recently announced that they are perfecting a maternal blood test that will permit technologists to map the entire genome of the developing fetus. Unlike amniocentesis, which requires the insertion of a needle into the womb to obtain amniotic fluid, the test would come earlier in the pregnancy and put the fetus at no risk—unless that is, it reveals unwanted genetic conditions or propensities. In such cases, the fetus's very life would suddenly be at material and immediate risk.

In a culture in which all people are valued equally regardless of their health or capacities, fetal genetic testing would be a splendid way to reveal the need for prenatal treatments or to allow parents time to prepare for a child with special needs. That's precisely how Todd and Sarah Palin reacted when the learned their youngest child Trig has Down syndrome. Long before he was born, they absorbed the emotional shock and then joyfully welcomed their son with open arms.

But such unconditional love cuts against the current cultural zeitgeist of our times. Consider: About 90 percent of fetuses testing for genetic conditions such as Down and dwarfism are terminated to the moral support, if not outright cheering, of much of society. It may seem harsh to say, but it is true nonetheless: We are in the midst of a great eugenic cleansing in which diagnosed imperfection often favors abortion.

There may even be overt pressure on parents to terminate from friends, family, and the medical community. The anti "defectives" message is vividly clear. When news came out in 2008 about the birth of Trig, Dr. André Lalonde, executive vice-president of the Society of Obstetricians and Gynecologists of Canada, groused that it could dissuade women from terminating, telling the *Globe and Mail*, "The worry is that this will have an implication for abortion issues in Canada." After studies showed that genetic counselors most often push women toward abortion when their fetuses test positive for Down, the late Ted Kennedy (D, MA) and Sam Brownback (R, KS) jointly authored a bill requiring "neutrality" in genetic counseling. Meanwhile, an Oregon jury recently awarded a couple $2.9 million after learning that the parents would have aborted their Down daughter but for botched prenatal testing.

Eugenic abortion is only part of the problem. Embryos created through IVF are often genetically tested before implantation, with the genetically unwanted thrown out as mere medical waste or turned over to biotechnologists for rending and research. True, some of these tests seek to prevent terrible diseases such as Huntington's. But some embryos have been destroyed because they have a genetic propensity to *adult* onset cancer. We have also seen IVF clinics advertising to cull embryos for purely cosmetic reasons, such as hair color. Sex selection embryo sorting and abortion are now a reality. The list goes on and on.

A cultural expectation is forming in which people believe they not only have a fundamental right to have a baby, but the concomitant right to have the *baby they want*—and by any technological means necessary. Worse, with genetic tests growing ever more sophisticated the potential that the fertility industrial complex will one day offer special order *Gattaca*-type babies is very real. (*Gattaca* depicts a future in which genetic engineering of embryos is universal and people considered genetically inferior are relegated to the fringes of society.)

The Decline in Down Syndrome

Down syndrome is the most common chromosomal abnormality, occurring in 1 in 691 births in the U.S. But, owing to prenatal testing, births of babies with Down syndrome are much less common than they use to be. A British study found that the number dropped 21 percent between 1989 and 2003. And a 2012 Danish study showed that the introduction of a national prenatal screening program halved the number of babies born with Down syndrome. Keep in mind, these declines occurred even as more women began to delay childbirth past age 35, after which women are appreciably more likely to conceive a child with Down. (The British study estimated that the number of women conceiving children with Down grew 51 percent.)

Declines in the U.S. have been less severe but no less astonishing. In 2004, researchers estimated that in the absence of prenatal diagnosis and abortion, Down syndrome births would have increased 56 percent between 1989 and 2001. Instead, they decreased by 7.8 percent.

Daniel Allott and George Neumayr,
"Eugenic Abortion 2.0: A New Blood Test Could
Zero Out the Disabled Unborn in the 21st Century,"
American Spectator, *May 2013.*

Missing in the eugenics quest for perfection are the many significant would-have-been contributors to society we might prevent from being born. Indeed, we can easily trace who could have been lost had our contemporary technological prowess been developed a few hundred years earlier. Beethoven might never have born considering his destined deafness. If Lincoln was bi-polar or had the genetic condition known as Marfan's syndrome, as some have speculated, he might well have been "selected out" in the hope that Tom and Nancy

Lincoln's next baby would have a less troubled nature. For that matter, the embryonic Winston Churchill might have been terminated when his genetic screeners warned his parents that he would have a predisposition for alcoholism. Similarly, Mother Teresa might have never been born had her parents known she would be diminutive and plain. Ditto Toulouse-Lautrec. And what if homosexuality turns out to have a determinable genetic component? There might never have been an Oscar Wilde.

Think about the everyday people whose absences would make our lives so much less full: The wise-cracking waitress with the club foot who makes Saturday morning breakfasts such a joy; the teacher whose students laugh at her speech impairment behind her back only to discover later that she changed their lives; the developmentally disabled man whose loving and selfless nature makes him the community favorite; the devoted father, like the late journalist and Bush Press Secretary (and my good friend) Tony Snow, who gave so much to his family and society before dying far too young from genetically-implicated colon cancer.

What a bitter irony. We claim to extol diversity and tolerance more than at any other time in human history—as we unleash a merciless reproductive pogrom to eradicate imperfection from the human condition.

That's a crying shame. If I were to pick one human attribute to extol above all others, it wouldn't be high intelligence, good looks, or athletic prowess—the usual targets for human improvement. Rather, I believe the most crucial human attribute is our capacity to love.

Nearly 2000 years ago, St. Paul wrote, "And now abide faith, hope, and love, these three; but the greatest of these is love." Who among us exhibit a greater unconditional love capacity than our brothers and sisters with Down syndrome? To the extent that they and other "defectives" are unwelcome among us can be measured our own deficiencies as a society.

> *"Perhaps more women are using prenatal testing for the purpose of preparation—medically and emotionally—rather than as a route towards termination."*

Prenatal Testing Does Not Necessarily Lead to More Abortion

Amy Julia Becker

In the following viewpoint, Amy Julia Becker recounts her own experience with prenatal testing and giving birth to a daughter with Down syndrome as illustrative of how both testing and society have changed. Becker claims that prenatal testing has always had the purpose of giving women the option to abort. Nonetheless, she contends that even with more advanced testing, the rate of abortion for Down syndrome is declining due to social progress for people with disabilities. Becker is author of What Every Woman Needs to Know About Prenatal Testing: Insight from a Mom Who Has Been There.

As you read, consider the following questions:

1. According to the author, why did she decide not to undergo amniocentesis to get a more definitive diagnosis when she was pregnant?

2. The new noninvasive blood tests can diagnose Down syndrome with what rate of accuracy, according to Becker?

3. What two pieces of legislation does the author claim have led to greater rights for those who live with disabilities?

In 2005, when I was pregnant with my first child, I was offered a "quad screen." A simple blood test that would identify a series of statistical probabilities that my baby had Down syndrome, other (less common) genetic diseases, or a neural tube defect.

A Personal Prenatal Testing Experience

I didn't think much of the test. It seemed like an easy way to learn about the life growing within me, and I assumed the results would allow me to cross a few worries off the list. I certainly didn't think about the intersection of historical, ethical, and economic concerns that had led to that moment.

But then the results came, and my doctor called to say that I had a 1 in 316 chance of having a child with Down syndrome—higher than the average 28-year-old "age-related risk" of 1 in 1000. Since my husband and I did not want the option of abortion, my doctor counseled us against an amniocentesis, which would have offered a definitive diagnosis, but would have also carried a slight risk that I would miscarry (1 in 200 to 400, depending upon the study). Instead, she suggested a Level Two Ultrasound.

The ultrasound technician measured our child's tibia and fibula and nuchal [back of the neck] fold, and did a prolonged search for other markers of trisomy 21 [an extra (third) chromosome 21], and then she pronounced: "This child may be many things. But it does not have Down syndrome." I promptly returned to a state of giddy excitement for the life ahead.

In retrospect I wonder why I spent so much time convincing myself that the test results would be negative. I spent no time thinking about why the prospect of a child with Down syndrome caused such tightness in my chest, such a need to convince myself that it couldn't be true of my child or within my family. Why was I so frightened of Down syndrome? Was it the way the tests were presented, the aura of somber intensity that came along with the uncertain results? Was it fear on behalf of my baby? Or fear for myself? Did it disrupt a hazy vision of the life I had always expected our family to lead? Was it the fact that a diagnosis of Down syndrome automatically led to a conversation about abortion, that Down syndrome automatically led to a choice that wouldn't have otherwise been on the table? I didn't ask myself any of those questions back then. I just wanted a healthy baby.

Our daughter Penny was born a few months later, and two hours after birth a pediatrician and neonatologist offered the unexpected news that she had Down syndrome after all. At the same time, she was healthy. But back then, "healthy" and "Down syndrome" didn't seem to belong in the same sentence.

Prenatal Testing and Abortion

In the eight years since I was pregnant with Penny, the prenatal testing landscape has changed significantly, but the questions women must address in choosing their course through prenatal tests haven't. Medical professionals have wanted to offer women the option of abortion for fetuses with "deformities" or "disabilities" for nearly a century, and women have wanted those options in light of the medical and social difficulties that can arise with a child with a disability.

As early as the 1930s, doctors who were arguing for legalized abortion used the prospect of aborting fetuses with "deformities" as a rationale for abortion in the case of medical necessity. As Daniel Williams, an associate professor of history at the University of West Georgia explained to me, "The belief that women should have the right to terminate pregnancies in which they suspected fetal deformities predated ultrasounds and prenatal testing. Those medical technologies certainly facilitated abortions, but the relationship between suspected fetal deformity and abortion preceded those tests by several decades . . . concerns about fetal deformity were driving the debate over abortion legalization even in the early 1960s, several years before ultrasounds were introduced."

Although prenatal testing did not exist in the form it does today, the desire to identify physical and intellectual fetal abnormalities contributed to the eventual legalization of abortion state by state and on a federal level.

Advances in Prenatal Testing

In more recent years, with the advent of ultrasound technology, amniocentesis, and prenatal screening tests, more and more women have been able to identify fetuses with atypical characteristics in utero. Ultrasound technology emerged in the 1960s, though it was not used in a routine manner until the 1980s. Blood tests that offered a probability of a fetus having Down syndrome or other conditions emerged in the late 1980s, and again, the link between these tests and abortion continued. In the past, definitive diagnosis of chromosomal conditions could only come via chorionic villa sampling (CVS) or amniocentesis, both procedures that pose some risk to the life of the fetus. As a result, doctors and women always considered the risk of miscarriage or harm to the fetus, and many women who didn't want the option of abortion declined the tests.

Now women can choose a noninvasive blood test, which researchers claim can diagnose Down syndrome and other trisomies during the first trimester of pregnancy with 99 percent accuracy. (Doctors still recommend a follow up diagnostic test, which is 99.99 percent accurate.)

As Erika Check Hayden wrote for *Nature*, "Observers expect the advantages of the non-invasive tests to expand the pool of women who opt for prenatal genetic screening in the United States each year from fewer than 100,000 to as many as 3 million." These new tests bring up the same ethical questions that have existed around abortion and genetic conditions for years, and yet they do so in an unprecedented way because the test is both safe and available early in pregnancy.

A Decline in Abortion for Down Syndrome

Currently somewhere between 70 and 85 percent of women in the United States with a prenatal diagnosis of Down syndrome choose abortion. But even though prenatal testing has advanced in accuracy and availability, the number of women who aborted used to be higher. Perhaps more women are using prenatal testing for the purpose of preparation—medically and emotionally—rather than as a route towards termination.

The same liberal social forces that led to the legalization of abortion forty years ago have also led to social progress for many individuals with disabilities, including those with Down syndrome. Due to legislation such as the Americans with Disabilities Act (ADA) and Individuals with Disabilities Education Act (IDEA, and its predecessor, The Education for All Handicapped Children Act), children and adults with disabilities have rights they never before could have imagined. Medical advances have also led to significant gains for individuals with Down syndrome. In the past thirty years, their life expectancy has doubled. With Early Intervention and inclusion in schools and other social settings, individuals with Down syndrome have also made cognitive gains that have led to greater independence as adults.

Certainly people with Down syndrome and other genetic conditions still suffer social stigma and physical difficulties. But life for a person with Down syndrome has never been more promising than it is today. Knowing the personal reality now that I didn't seven years ago—of a daughter who loves reading, who squabbles with her little brother and tries to take care of her little sister, and has braces on her ankles and glasses on her nose and loves to dance—I've come to see that my fears were largely unfounded.

Recent demand has led to market gains for biotechnology companies like Sequenom, which developed the blood test to detect Down's syndrome, and most insurers cover prenatal screening and subsequent diagnostic tests. So it is in the midst of these historical, economic, and medical forces that parents must consider the proper place for these tests in offering the information they need to care for their children.

Periodical and Internet Sources Bibliography

The following articles have been selected to supplement the diverse views presented in this chapter.

Lindsay Abrams	"Prenatal Testing: Earlier and More Accurate than Ever," *Atlantic Monthly*, November 5, 2012.
Daniel Allott and George Neumayr	"Eugenic Abortion 2.0," *American Spectator*, May 2013.
Marcy Darnovsky	"One Step Closer to Designer Babies: New Noninvasive Prenatal Genetic Testing Could Change Human Pregnancy Forever," Science Progress, April 22, 2011. www.scienceprogress.org.
Charles A. Donovan	"Testing Ourselves: Researchers Simplify Prenatal Genetic Scans," *National Review*, June 7, 2012.
Ricki Lewis	"Prenatal Genetic Testing: When Is It 'Toxic Knowledge'?," *DNA Science Blog*, October 18, 2012. www.blogs.plos.org/dnascience.
Jane Parry	"Screening the Genes: Low- and Middle-Income Countries Are Catching Up on the Use of Screening for Birth Defects," *Bulletin of the World Health Organization*, August 2012.
Bonnie Rochman	"Why Cheaper Genetic Testing Could Cost Us a Fortune," *Time*, October 26, 2012.
Jennifer B. Saunders	"Screening Newborns for Heart Defects," *State Legislatures*, December 2012.
David Shenk	"The Limits of Genetic Testing," *Atlantic Monthly*, April 3, 2012.

OPPOSING
VIEWPOINTS®
SERIES

CHAPTER 4

How Should Birth Defects Be Addressed?

Chapter Preface

The issue of what should be done about birth defects includes questions of prevention, termination of pregnancy (and even infanticide, as debated in this chapter), and treatment; however, part of the question of what to do about birth defects entails a careful look at the various conditions defined as birth defects and the extent to which certain abnormalities are deemed to be problems or merely differences. In recent years, controversy surrounding congenital deafness illustrates the importance of the normative assumptions made about birth defects.

Hearing impairment is one of the most common congenital abnormalities. Approximately 3 in 1,000 babies born in the United States each year, about 12,000, are born with some kind of hearing impairment. About 25 percent of children born with hearing loss also have other birth defects, such as cerebral palsy. The US Centers for Disease Control and Prevention reports that researchers believe genetics are responsible for about half of the cases of hearing impairment, although it is thought that multiple genes are involved. About 90 percent of babies born with congenital hearing impairment are born to parents with normal hearing, and almost 90 percent of children born to deaf parents are able to hear.

Although deafness is widely considered a congenital abnormality, or birth defect, there are those who disagree with this terminology and the assumptions it makes. Many within the deaf community find the language of defect and disability to be insulting and inaccurate. In its statement on the use of cochlear implants, which are often the treatment recommended for babies born with severe hearing impairment, the National Association of the Deaf says:

> Many within the medical profession continue to view deafness essentially as a disability and an abnormality and be-

lieve that deaf and hard of hearing individuals need to be "fixed" by cochlear implants. This pathological view must be challenged and corrected by greater exposure to and interaction with well-adjusted and successful deaf and hard of hearing individuals.

If deafness is not a disability, then there is nothing to be fixed, either before or after birth. An extreme version of this view was seen in the United Kingdom several years ago when a deaf couple wanted to use *in vitro* fertilization, a reproductive technology, to purposely select for a deaf child. Their desire caused an uproar, but they argued that deafness was not a disability but simply a difference.

Yet, some see this attempt to define deafness simply as a difference to be disingenuous, denying the reality of living with hearing impairment. Australian professor of sign language linguistics, Trevor Johnston, in "In One's Own Image: Ethics and the Reproduction of Deafness," notes:

> Deafness is a disability (albeit with its own special features such as a cultural and linguistic dimension) because there is a real loss of expected function and, thus, as with any unwanted disabling condition, it is considered right and proper for individuals, medical science, and the society as a whole to act to avoid it.

As Johnston alludes, the very concept of disability has within it the notion of something lost or missing. If deafness is a disability, then, it is something that warrants treatment or avoidance.

The debate about deafness illustrates that the terminology used regarding birth defects, or congenital abnormalities, contains within it some sense of what is to be done about it. Defects are generally assumed to be problematic and to be corrected. But as we see with deafness, there is neither agreement about which conditions constitute birth defects nor about what needs to be done about certain conditions. The viewpoints in this chapter debate various responses to what should be done in such cases.

| *"You'd have to be very, very well trained in ethics to see the authors' argument as a morally acceptable extension of their premises, but . . . [for] the rest of us . . . [it is] self-evident absurdity."*

The Argument That It Is Morally Permissible to Kill Defective Newborns Is Absurd

Andrew Ferguson

In the following viewpoint, Andrew Ferguson objects to the argument that after-birth abortion, or the killing of newborns, should be seen as morally permissible. Ferguson expresses outrage at the argument by two medical ethicists that parents should be allowed to kill an infant who has minor physical disabilities or who is simply unwanted. Ferguson suggests that the fact that such an outrageous argument rests on the permissibility of abortion says a lot about the moral permissibility of abortion. Ferguson is senior editor of the Weekly Standard *and a columnist for* Bloomberg News.

As you read, consider the following questions:

1. According to Ferguson, what is the professional specialty of the medical ethicist?

Andrew Ferguson, "Declaring War on Newborns: The Disgrace of Medical Ethics," *Weekly Standard*, vol. 17, no. 26, March 19, 2012. Copyright © 2012 by The Weekly Standard. All rights reserved. Reproduced by permission.

2. The author draws an analogy between the after-birth abortion argument and what eighteenth-century satirical essay?

3. What does Ferguson think about the logic of the argument in favor of after-birth abortion?

On the list of the world's most unnecessary occupations—aromatherapist, golf pro, journalism professor, vice president of the United States—that of medical ethicist ranks very high. They are happily employed by pharmaceutical companies, hospitals, and other outposts of the vast medical-industrial combine, where their job is to advise the boss to go ahead and do what he was going to do anyway ("Put it on the market!" "Pull the plug on the geezer!"). They also attend conferences where they take turns sitting on panels talking with one another and then sitting in the audience watching panels of other medical ethicists talking with one another. Their professional specialty is the "thought experiment," which is the best kind of experiment because you don't have to buy test tubes or leave the office. And sometimes they get jobs at universities, teaching other people to become ethicists. It is a cozy, happy world they live in.

But it was painfully roiled last month [February 2012], when a pair of medical ethicists took to their profession's bible, the *Journal of Medical Ethics*, and published an essay with a misleadingly inconclusive title: "After-birth Abortion: Why should the baby live?" It was a misleading title because the authors believe the answer to the question is: "Beats me."

Right at the top, the ethicists summarized the point of their article. "What we call 'after-birth abortion' (killing a newborn) should be permissible in all the cases where abortion is, including cases where the newborn is not disabled."

The Argument for After-Birth Abortion

The argument made by the authors—Alberto Giubilini and Francesca Minerva, both of them affliliated with prestigious universities in Australia and ethicists of pristine reputations—runs as follows. Let's suppose a woman gets pregnant. She decides to go ahead and have the baby on the assumption that her personal circumstances, and her views on such things as baby-raising, will remain the same through the day she gives birth and beyond.

Then she gives birth. Perhaps the baby is disabled or suffers a disease. Perhaps her boyfriend or (if she's old-fashioned) her husband abandons her, leaving her in financial peril. Or perhaps she's decided that she's just not the mothering kind, for, as the authors write, "having a child can itself be an unbearable burden for the psychological health of the woman or for her already existing children, regardless of the condition of the fetus."

The authors point out that each of these conditions—the baby is sick or suffering, the baby will be a financial hardship, the baby will be personally troublesome—is now "largely accepted" as a good reason for a mother to abort her baby before he's born. So why not after?

"When circumstances occur *after birth* such that they would have justified abortion, what we call *after-birth abortion* should be permissible." (Their italics.) Western societies approve abortion because they have reached a consensus that a fetus is not a person; they should acknowledge that by the same definition a newborn isn't a person either. Neither fetus nor baby has developed a sufficient sense of his own life to know what it would be like to be deprived of it. The kid will never know the difference, in other words. A newborn baby is just a fetus who's hung around a bit too long.

As the authors acknowledge, this makes an "after-birth abortion" a tricky business. You have to get to the infant before he develops "those properties that justify the attribution of a right to life to an individual." It's a race against time.

A Multitude of Surprising Conclusions

The article doesn't go on for more than 1,500 words, but for non-ethicists it has a high surprise-per-word ratio. The information that newborn babies aren't people is just the beginning. A reader learns that "many non-human animals . . . are persons" and therefore enjoy a "right to life." (Such ruminative ruminants, unlike babies, are self-aware enough to know that getting killed will entail a "loss of value.") The authors don't tell us which species these "non-human persons" belong to, but it's safe to say that you don't want to take a medical ethicist to dinner at Outback.

But what about adoption, you ask. The authors ask that question too, noting that some people—you and me, for example—might think that adoption could buy enough time for the unwanted newborn to technically become a person and "possibly increase the happiness of the people involved." But this is not a viable option, if you'll forgive the expression. A mother who kills her newborn baby, the authors report, is forced to "accept the irreversibility of the loss." By contrast, a mother who gives her baby up for adoption "might suffer psychological distress." And for a very simple reason: These mothers "often dream that their child will return to them. This makes it difficult to accept the reality of the loss because they can never be quite sure whether or not it is irreversible." It's simpler for all concerned just to make sure the loss can't be reversed. It'll spare Mom a lot of heartbreak.

Now, it's at this point in the *Journal of Medical Ethics* that many readers will begin to suspect, as I did, that their legs are being not very subtly pulled. The inversion that the argument entails is Swiftian—a twenty-first-century "Modest Proposal" without the cannibalism (for now). Jonathan Swift's original "Modest Proposal" called for killing Irish children to prevent them "from being a burden to their parents." It was death by compassion, the killing of innocents based on a surfeit of

The Slippery Slope Argument

The slippery slope argument has long been scorned by the liberal left, who adamantly denied that born human beings would also eventually be subject to death sentences handed out to the unborn. Preposterous, the left cried. A logical fallacy! Never would happen! "B" does not follow "A"!

But [Alberto] Giubilini and [Francesca] Minerva have used the slippery slope argument in *favor* of infanticide.

There are, after all, the good doctors argue, abnormalities which cannot be detected until after birth. Such deformities render the child's life "not worth living."

Fay Voshell, "Infanticide on Demand,"
AmericanThinker.com, March 1, 2012.

fellow-feeling. The authors agree that compassion itself demands the death of newborns. Unlike Swift, though, they aren't kidding.

They get you coming and going, these guys. They assume—and they won't get much argument from their peers in the profession—that "mentally impaired" infants are eligible for elimination because they will never develop the properties necessary to be fully human. Then they discuss Treacher-Collins syndrome, which causes facial deformities and respiratory ailments but no mental impairment. Kids with TCS are "fully aware of their condition, of being different from other people and of all the problems their pathology entails," and are therefore, to spare them a life of such unpleasant awareness, eligible for elimination too—because they are *not* mentally impaired. The threshold to this "right to life" just gets higher and higher, the more you think about it.

A Thought Experiment

And of course it is their business to think about it. It's what medical ethicists get paid to do: cogitate, cogitate, cogitate. As "After-birth Abortion" spread around the world and gained wide publicity—that damned Internet—non-ethicists greeted it with derision or shock or worse. The authors and the editor of the *Journal of Medical Ethics* were themselves shocked at the response. As their inboxes flooded with hate mail, the authors composed an apology of sorts that non-ethicists will find more revealing even than the original paper.

"We are really sorry that many people, who do not share the background of the intended audience for this article, felt offended, outraged, or even threatened," they wrote. "The article was supposed to be read by other fellow bioethicists who were already familiar with this topic and our arguments." It was a *thought experiment*. After all, among medical ethicists "this debate"—about when it's proper to kill babies—"has been going on for 40 years."

So *that's* what they've been talking about in all those panel discussions! The authors thought they were merely taking the next step in a train of logic that was set in motion, and has been widely accepted, since their profession was invented in the 1960s. And of course they were. The outrage directed at their article came from laymen—people unsophisticated in contemporary ethics. Medical ethicists in general expressed few objections, only a minor annoyance that the authors had let the cat out of the bag. A few days after it was posted the article was removed from the publicly accessible area of the *Journal's* website, sending it back to that happy, cozy world.

The Logic of the Argument

You'd have to be very, very well trained in ethics to see the authors' argument as a morally acceptable extension of their premises, but you can't deny the logic of it. The rest of us will see in the argument an extension of its premises into self-evident absurdity. Pro-lifers should take note. For years, in public argument, pro-choicers have mocked them for not following their belief in a fetus's humanity to its logical end. *Shouldn't you execute doctors who perform abortions? Why don't you have funerals for miscarriages?*

As one pro-choice wag [Michael Kinsley], writing about the Republicans' pro-life platform, put it in the *Washington Post* a few years ago: "The official position of the Republican Party is that women who have abortions should be executed."

And now we know the pro-choice position is that children born with a facial deformity should be executed too, as long as you get to them quick enough. Unwittingly the insouciant authors of "After-birth Abortion" have shown where pro-choicers wind up if they follow *their* belief about fetuses to its logical end. They've performed a public service. Could it be that medical ethicists really are more useful than aromatherapists?

| *"Younger women should be getting more amnio than older ones."*

Amniocentesis Should Be Offered More Regularly to Younger Pregnant Women

Ray Fisman

In the following viewpoint, Ray Fisman argues that the standard recommendation that primarily older women should get prenatal screening through amniocentesis is misguided. Fisman cites a study suggesting that, in fact, the benefits of having the knowledge from amniocentesis may be greater for younger women and the costs of the tests higher for older women. Fisman claims that the new recommendations to discuss amniocentesis with all pregnant women are often not followed. Fisman is the codirector of the Social Enterprise Program and a senior scholar at the Chazen Institute at the Columbia University Business School in New York City.

As you read, consider the following questions:

1. According to Fisman, what risk does prenatal screening with amniocentesis pose?

2. The author claims that the traditional recommendation regarding amniocentesis and age was developed in the mid-1970s by comparing what two risks?

3. According to Fisman, a 2008 survey of obstetricians found that what percentage recommended amniocentesis to their patients under thirty-five?

When my wife became pregnant with our first child in early 2007, we discovered the joys—and the anxieties—that accompany parenthood even before a baby is born. For better or worse, modern medicine has taken some of the guesswork out of preparing for a child—you can determine gender (pink or blue crib sheets?), resolve questions of paternity, and test for the many things that can and occasionally do go wrong in a fetus's development. Even if prenatal testing doesn't allow the parents-in-waiting to sleep much better at night, it affords them the opportunity to plan for what's in store and to make better-informed choices on the most fraught of decisions: whether to continue the pregnancy to term.

The Standard Recommendation

But the testing regimen can itself be a source of anxiety, with some procedures presenting a risk to the fetus. And for such a high-stakes decision, medical science's assessment of the trade-offs involved can be rather unscientific. For one common prenatal test, amniocentesis, the common recommendation that women over the age of 35 should have the test may not only be unscientific, but exactly backward. The 35-year rule, it turns out, was based on a fallacy in reasoning that might have you questioning other treatment protocols on your next visit to the doctor's office.

Amniocentesis, a common screen at the end of the first trimester, involves the insertion of a needle into the uterus to extract a couple of tablespoons' worth of the amniotic fluid that surrounds the developing fetus. Lab tests on the extracted fluid provide a clear indication of whether the unborn child has Down syndrome or other genetic abnormalities. But the procedure carries with it an increased probability of miscarriage in the weeks that follow.

Is it worth risking a carefully nurtured fetus for information on an unborn child's genetic destiny? At the time my wife and I began to ask such questions, standard obstetric practice was that amnio or its alternative, chorionic villus sampling, be offered automatically to any woman over 35, but not to younger women without specific risk factors like a family history of genetic disorders. On the face of it, an age cutoff makes sense—fetuses of older women are at higher risk of genetic defects—and one would expect that the 35-year cutoff was developed on the basis of sound scientific evaluation.

The Costs and Benefits of Amniocentesis

It stands to reason that a woman should get amnio if the benefits of amnio exceed its costs. The clinical doctrine of testing after 35 would imply that the costs of amnio outweigh the benefits for younger women, but around age 35, the benefits begin to exceed the costs.

What are these costs and benefits? The cost is the increased probability of miscarriage from fluid extraction. (This higher risk is thought to be fairly similar for women of all ages.) The benefit of amnio is discovering genetic defects, the chances of which accelerate with age—the odds that a 20-year-old woman will give birth to a Down syndrome baby is a little under 1 in 2,000; this doubles by the time she's 32, and it's nearly 10 times higher by 38. There is similarly a steep increase in prevalence of other genetic abnormalities. So, for two otherwise comparable women—with likeminded attitudes toward abortion, comparable incomes, and similar family sizes—it seems reasonable to suggest that the one with a tenfold higher risk would get a bigger benefit from testing.

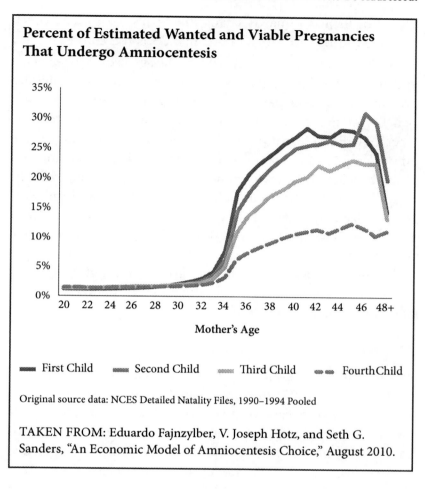

Percent of Estimated Wanted and Viable Pregnancies That Undergo Amniocentesis

Mother's Age

First Child   Second Child   Third Child   Fourth Child

Original source data: NCES Detailed Natality Files, 1990–1994 Pooled

TAKEN FROM: Eduardo Fajnzylber, V. Joseph Hotz, and Seth G. Sanders, "An Economic Model of Amniocentesis Choice," August 2010.

But why 35? The cutoff was first developed in the mid-1970s, based on estimates that the miscarriage risk from amnio was 1 in 200. For women under 35, this was greater than the odds of giving birth to a child with Down syndrome. For women older than 35, the ever-increasing probability of Down and other genetic defects was such that it exceeded this 1-in-200 threshold. The 35+ rule became firmly entrenched clinical gospel—in 2007 (just as new rules on genetic screening were announced), the *New York Times* quoted Dr. Deborah Driscoll, chairwoman of the obstetrics department at the University of Pennsylvania, as saying that "[i]t's been pretty much ingrained in obstetricians' minds that 35 is the cutoff age."

As far back as the early 1990s, though, some physicians and decision scientists have voiced concerns that probabilities are only one small part of comparing the overall costs and benefits of miscarriage versus testing. You also need to consider how badly a couple wishes to conceive (and hence the emotional toll of a second trimester miscarriage), as compared with the usefulness of learning of potential fetal abnormalities. It's a very difficult and highly personal comparison. Narrowly following a 35+ rule caused many older women who really, really wanted to have kids to get amnio when they probably shouldn't have. Meanwhile, many younger women— ones who felt strongly about not carrying through to the delivery of a child with genetic abnormalities—likely should have gotten amnio but didn't.

The New Recommendations

As my wife and I pondered these personal questions for ourselves back in 2007, the American College of Obstetricians and Gynecologists came out with a new set of guidelines, recommending that obstetricians discuss the pros and cons of amnio with *all* women, regardless of age. But old diagnostic habits die hard—a 2008 survey of obstetricians found that more than 90 percent were still recommending amnio to their over-35 patients, but for under-35s, the figure was only 15 percent. Amnio FAQ sites from respected sources like the Mayo Clinic still list 35 as a cutoff for recommending the test.

I was prompted to write this column when I came across a study by a trio of economists arguing that the 35-year cutoff isn't merely arbitrary, it's backward—that is, younger women should be getting *more* amnio than older ones. They argue that the cost of miscarriage to a woman in her late 30s— facing down the childbearing limits imposed by menopause—is far higher than it is for a 20-year-old with many childbearing years ahead of her. Though the chances of genetic abnormality spiral upward with age, the chances of successfully conceiving a child spiral downward even faster.

The authors aren't so bold as to suggest their own age-dependent rule—they acknowledge that prenatal diagnostic choices should depend on personal circumstances and that women should be counseled accordingly. But this counsel should include a more forward-looking view of the effects of an amnio-induced miscarriage.

It's only natural that we crave black-and-white rules, ones that provide clear, unambiguous prescriptions. The current guidelines offer flexibility by providing doctors and patients with relevant information yet allowing them to decide based on individual circumstance. But the guidelines also present an overwhelming array of testing options and considerations that—judging from the persistence of the 35+ rule—makes doctors and patients alike long for the old days of simple treatment rules, whether or not they're right.

> "Advancements in treatment offer spina bifida patients far greater hope . . . but other medical advancements . . . coupled with abortion on demand, mean that a child with this birth defect will likely be aborted before any of these new procedures can be tried."

Birth Defects Should Not Necessarily Result in Abortion

Steve Hall

In the following viewpoint, Steve Hall recounts his own experience with spina bifida in support of his argument that fetuses with birth defects should not be aborted. Hall claims that despite the poor prognosis the doctors gave to his mother, he has lived a full life. He claims that the situation for people born with spina bifida now is even better than at the time he was born, but he contends that most people choose to abort fetuses with spina bifida, a situation that he finds lamentable and frightening. Hall is an attorney and a theologian in Virginia.

As you read, consider the following questions:

1. Which US Supreme Court decision does the author claim is responsible for fewer babies being born with spina bifida?

2. The author claims that his mother refused surgeries for his spina bifida because they carried how high of a risk of death?

3. Hall contends that prior to the Nazi genocide of Jews, the Nazis were killing what two groups of people?

I was born in 1965 with spina bifida, a birth defect that affects the development of the spine and lower extremities. It can vary in its severity—and my case is less severe than many—but in the mid-1960s, nearly all spina bifida cases were considered severe and many affected babies did not survive. You would think that because of medical advances, children five decades later would have a greater chance of survival—and they do—but those advancements are often of little benefit, thanks to a single Supreme Court decision: *Roe v. Wade* [1973].

The Treatment of Spina Bifida

By God's grace, I was born to a loving but determined mother who was also a nurse. She allowed doctors to perform needed exploratory surgery on me the day I was born. During that operation, my heart stopped on the operating table. To the shock of many, the doctor restarted my heart with epinephrine. Back then children with my "disability" were often left to die in such circumstances. My mom believed it was because of a greater plan God had for me.

Even though I survived that operation, doctors thought I would be unable to care for myself and would depend on others my entire life. My parents were also told I needed additional surgeries—procedures that carried an 80 percent risk of death. As a nurse, and by asking the right questions, Mom knew I might not need those operations, so she refused to allow them—a decision that proved to be correct but also got us kicked out of the hospital that was treating me.

Today, advancements in treatment offer spina bifida patients far greater hope for mobility and improved "quality of life." Some corrective surgeries can now be performed before birth. But other medical advancements, including the ability to detect spina bifida before birth, coupled with abortion on demand, mean that a child with this birth defect will likely be aborted before any of these new procedures can be tried. In fact, one widely quoted study found that 64 percent of unborn babies diagnosed with spina bifida in the United States and in several other Western countries are aborted.

Proving the Predictions Incorrect

My parents sacrificed greatly to provide the best care they could find throughout my childhood. Mom, in particular, spent months in various hospitals with me. It was during a particularly long, four-month hospital stay I came to Christ.

I also faced challenges in school, where I was the first "disabled" child in our local public school system during my elementary years. I got through those trials, was admitted to college a year early, and then went on to seminary and law school. My parents attended all those graduations, where the predictions from my first few months of life were proven incorrect.

I'm now an attorney and lived independently until I married a lovely woman several years ago. I've served as a deacon and an elder in two churches and am grateful for many years of memories with my (now late) parents, my brother and his family, and many friends.

The Quality-of-Life Argument

I suppose my "quality of life" turned out much better than my early doctors expected. That is due to God's grace, much of it shown through the love and care of my parents, who even after *Roe v. Wade* would have chosen life for me.

But the quality-of-life argument for opposing abortion misses the larger point: All life is God-given, and we should protect it to the extent we can, no matter how much a person proves to contribute to society. The way we treat "the least of these" and other vulnerable members of society is a test of us individually and as a nation.

We forget that the Nazis first practiced their killing techniques on the disabled and elderly before turning their fatal craft on the Jews. The German church rallied to stop the slaughter of the disabled during those early days of the Third Reich. If only we would now.

> "*Legal protections have not always brought with them the anticipated acceptance of having a child with disabilities.*"

Social Norms Must Follow Law in Acceptance of People with Disabilities

Dov Fox and Christopher L. Griffin Jr.

In the following viewpoint, Dov Fox and Christopher L. Griffin Jr. argue that although the Americans with Disabilities Act (ADA) has enhanced legal protections for people with birth defects and other disabilities, the law has not changed public opinion about disabled people. The authors claim that statistics show that fewer babies with Down syndrome have been born since passage of the ADA, suggesting a need for a change in social norms. Fox is an assistant professor at the University of San Diego School of Law and Griffin is an assistant professor at William & Mary Law School.

As you read, consider the following questions:

1. By what percentage did Down syndrome birthrates fall after passage of the Americans with Disabilities Act, according to the authors?

2. What have been the "expressive externalities" of the Americans with Disabilities Act, according to Fox and Griffin?

3. According to the authors, research shows that prevailing biases can be dislodged in what way?

Doctors and advocates have recently argued that parents are increasingly willing to bring a pregnancy to term after a positive test for Down syndrome. They explain this change, in part, as the result of the landmark Americans with Disabilities Act (ADA), which Congress enacted to fight employment discrimination and enhance access to public accommodations. What they fail to appreciate is that these legal protections have not always brought with them the anticipated acceptance of having a child with disabilities.

The Law and Public Attitudes

A study we published in 2009 reveals a staggering 25 percent decline in Down syndrome birthrates nationwide *after* the first President Bush [i.e., George H.W.] signed the ADA into law. Controlling for medical, demographic, and technological variables from maternal age and marital status to abortion access and prenatal care, we found that about 15 fewer children per 100,000 were born with Down syndrome in the years after the law was passed, even as prenatal testing rates remained constant. It is true that newer methods like the "quad screen" are less intrusive than amniocentesis and more accurate than chorionic villa sampling in identifying fetal abnormalities. Yet our analysis shows the absence of any clear correlation between the quality or availability of prenatal screening and the incidence of Down syndrome births. The question remains: Why would *fewer* children be brought into the world just as they are being afforded *greater* opportunities in life?

Part of the explanation lies in the unexpected messages that civil rights legislation can convey—through salient media

Section 1630.4 of the ADA

(a) *In general*—(1) It is unlawful for a covered entity to discriminate on the basis of disability against a qualified individual in regard to:

(i) Recruitment, advertising, and job application procedures;

(ii) Hiring, upgrading, promotion, award of tenure, demotion, transfer, layoff, termination, right of return from layoff, and rehiring;

(iii) Rates of pay or any other form of compensation and changes in compensation;

(iv) Job assignments, job classifications, organizational structures, position descriptions, lines of progression, and seniority lists;

(v) Leaves of absence, sick leave, or any other leave;

(vi) Fringe benefits available by virtue of employment, whether or not administered by the covered entity;

(vii) Selection and financial support for training, including: apprenticeships, professional meetings, conferences and other related activities, and selection for leaves of absence to pursue training;

(viii) Activities sponsored by a covered entity, including social and recreational programs; and

(ix) Any other term, condition, or privilege of employment.

Americans with Disabilities Act, 1990.

and popular culture—to people vaguely familiar with the law or unaware it even exists. These "expressive externalities" arise from public reaction to the unforeseen costs of implementing laws like the ADA. Negative newspaper and television reports seeking to justify new disability protections, or bemoaning the cost of their implementation, can reinforce the anxiety that parents describe as they await genetic test results during pregnancy. They read over breakfast the recent report of local efforts to bar a boy with Down syndrome from playing on a high school basketball team. Or they watch on the evening news this story about another teen with Down syndrome who was kicked off a plane. Accounts like these underscore the power of expressive externalities to shore up ascriptions of blame for having a child with known disabilities.

The Entrenched Biases

Implicit association testing strongly suggests that the enduring derision of people with disabilities (and Down syndrome in particular) has seeped pervasively into the public consciousness. The encouraging takeaway from this research is that prevailing biases can be dislodged through exposure to more accurate information about people with disabilities. Even sitcoms can educate us. Take a single TV network like Fox. Uplifting depictions on *Glee* have the power to counteract a demeaning portrayal on *Family Guy*. We should not close our eyes to these larger social forces that lie behind the natural fears about raising a child with Down syndrome.

Parents have every right to know what to expect when they are expecting. Yet social norms can scare us into thinking the only "responsible" decision is to prevent the existence of the very class of people in need of the law's protection. We the People reaffirmed in 2008 our commitment to the civil rights of people with disabilities. Now we must address the bad social meanings that can follow good laws. The weight of empirical evidence makes clear the need for stronger efforts to offset the distorted public understandings of people with disabilities that persist.

> "[Americans United for Life] has developed model legislation banning abortions done solely for reasons of sex-selection or genetic abnormalities."

Abortions Performed Because of Genetic Abnormalities Should Be Banned

Denise M. Burke

In the following viewpoint, Denise M. Burke argues that abortion of fetuses because of sex selection or genetic abnormalities should be legally prohibited. Burke claims that sex-selection abortion occurs in the United States and is not outlawed nationwide. She contends that more accurate prenatal testing is causing people to test for gender or genetic abnormalities with the purpose of seeking abortion for fetuses with unwanted characteristics. Burke is vice president of legal affairs for Americans United for Life (AUL) and the editor in chief of AUL's annual publication, Defending Life.

As you read, consider the following questions:

1. According to Burke, what piece of legislation was proposed in 2012 to prohibit sex-selection abortions?

2. In what four situations does the author claim that prenatal testing is commonly used to identify genetic abnormalities?

3. Burke says that prenatal testing can be a valuable tool
for what purposes?

In recent years, the practice of sex-selection abortions has
drawn increasing attention worldwide. Sex-selection abortions are abortions undertaken to eliminate a child of an undesired sex, with the targeted victims of such abortions over-
whelmingly female. The problem is so severe in some countries
that, in 2005, the United Nations Population Fund (UNFPA)
termed the practice "female infanticide." In 2011, author Mara
Hvistendahl reported in her book, *Unnatural Selection*, that
163 million girls are missing in the world because of sex-
selection abortions.

The Problem of Sex-Selective Abortions

While the practice of sex-selection abortions is common in
some Asian countries, such as China and India, it is also being
practiced in the United States, often by people who trace their
ancestry to countries that commonly practice sex-selection
abortions. In 2012, the organization Live Action sent investigators into Planned Parenthood clinics around the country
and revealed that the abortion giant was willing to perform
sex-selection abortions—even later-term abortions, when the
risks to maternal health exponentially increase.

Lawmakers have begun focusing more attention on the
problem of sex-selection abortions, with states considering
and enacting prohibitions on sex-selection abortions. For example, in 2012, the U.S. House of Representatives considered
the "Prenatal Nondiscrimination Act of 2012" (PRENDA)
(H.R. 3541). PRENDA would have prohibited sex discrimina-

Sex-Selection Abortion Bans

Four states ban abortions targeted toward the gender of the child: AZ, IL, OK, and PA.

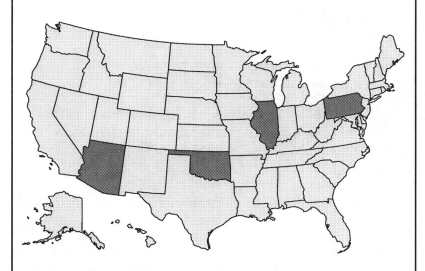

TAKEN FROM: Americans United for Life, "Ban on Abortions for Sex Selection and Genetic Abnormalities," 2012.

tion against an unborn child by proscribing the killing of the child based on his or her sex. A bipartisan majority of the House (246-168) voted in favor of PRENDA, but a two-thirds vote was necessary for passage.

Importantly, a 2012 poll by the Charlotte Lozier Institute found that 77 percent of Americans support prohibitions on abortions based solely on the sex of the unborn child.

The Use of Prenatal Testing

Moreover, prenatal testing is becoming increasingly common and many diagnostic tests are intended to provide parents and healthcare providers with information about an unborn baby's health and development (including the child's sex). Currently, prenatal testing to identify and diagnose potential genetic abnormalities or disorders is commonly used in cases where a pregnant woman:

- Is age 35 or older, because she is generally at higher risk for having a child with a chromosomal abnormality;

- Has a family history of an inherited condition such as Duchenne muscular dystrophy;

- Whose ancestry or ethnic background means that she might have a higher chance of an inherited disorder such as sickle cell anemia, thalassemia, or Tay-Sachs disease; or

- Is screened for common genetic disorders such as spina bifida and Down syndrome.

Two diagnostic procedures are common in prenatal testing: amniocentesis involves testing a sample of amniotic fluid from the womb, while chorionic villus sampling (CVS) involves taking a tiny tissue sample from outside the sac where the child is growing.

Genetic Abnormalities and Abortion

Prenatal testing can be a valuable tool for diagnosing and treating conditions that threaten the health or life of the mother, the child, or both. However, in some cases and despite documented error rates for the testing, it is also being used as a precursor for aborting a child of an undesired sex or with potential genetic abnormalities or defects. For example, recent studies have indicated that more than 90 percent of unborn children diagnosed with Down syndrome are aborted.

Clearly, this chilling slide toward eugenics—specifically, eliminating persons with certain hereditary characteristics— must be confronted. Notably, one of the most prominent

American supporters of eugenics was Margaret Sanger, the founder of Planned Parenthood.

AUL [Americans United for Life] has developed model legislation banning abortions done solely for reasons of sex-selection or genetic abnormalities such as Down syndrome.

> "All abortion is selective, and whether a woman has selected not to have a baby at all or has selected not to have a particular baby is not a matter the state should parse."

Women Should Be Able to Choose Abortion or Life When Faced with Fetal Abnormalities

Andrew Solomon

In the following viewpoint, Andrew Solomon argues that a North Dakota law banning abortion for the purpose of avoiding having a child with birth defects—among other restrictions—is misguided. Solomon claims that there is extreme rhetoric on both sides of the issue. He denies that all babies should be born and nurtured, whatever their abnormalities, but he also believes that pregnancy termination should be approached more thoughtfully in the case of birth defects. Regardless, he concludes that the ability to make the choice for oneself is most important. Solomon is an award-winning writer on politics, culture, and psychology.

As you read, consider the following questions:

1. According to Solomon, what kind of abortion does the North Dakota law he discusses prohibit?

2. How does each side of the debate pressure women pregnant with fetuses with disabilities, according to the author?

3. According to the author, approximately how many children with Down syndrome are born each year in the United States to women who had a prenatal diagnosis?

The abortion laws passed last week [March 26, 2013,] in North Dakota are troubling first and foremost because they restrict women's freedom to control their own bodies. More insidiously, they criminalize *selective abortion*, which means that a woman cannot choose to terminate a pregnancy because she knows the fetus has a genetic abnormality, or to select for other characteristics, such as gender. The very use of the world "selective" here indicates how right the pro-choice movement has been to emphasize "choice." All abortion is selective, and whether a woman has selected not to have a baby at all or has selected not to have a particular baby is not a matter the state should parse. No one should be forced to have a child she doesn't wish to have.

Problems from Both Sides

Both anti-abortionists and disability activists have sometimes suggested that women should defer to "nature" and have whatever baby they conceive. The bioethicist William Ruddick calls this the "'hospitality' view of women." The proposition is that we do not have and should not exercise volition in the making of children; pregnancies are an arranged marriage we are not free to buck. Yet a study [by Karen L. Lawson] a few years ago concluded that women who do not make use of prenatal testing or who choose to keep pregnancies they know will lead to children with disabilities "were judged more responsible, more to blame, and less deserving of both sympathy and social aid subsequent to giving birth to a disabled child than were women to whom testing was not made available." The hospitality view is oppressive, but so is the rush to social judgment.

I have written in my most recent book, "Far From the Tree," about the rich experience many parents find in children with conditions against which people often select. I would never propose to anyone—even to myself—that such parents' rapture constitutes an imperative to bring similar children into the world.

I do see a problem, however, in the speed with which women who have no prior exposure to the conditions in question are expected to make these decisions. Women often terminate a pregnancy without knowing what life would be like with and for an anomalous child. It is worth publicizing the satisfaction that the experience may entail, so that the pro-choice movement becomes the pro-*informed*-choice movement. Others have already pointed out that if we want people to keep these pregnancies, we might start by providing better services for people with disabilities; our neglect of decent care is a national disgrace, and is ignored in North Dakota's new statutes.

There is muddle from both sides on abortion after prenatal diagnosis. The women I interviewed, whether they had carried such children to term or had terminated, described intense pressure pushing them away from their natural inclination. The political right conflates choice and abortion, implying that most women will terminate, eliminating disabled populations whose lives have value. It also honeys the story of challenging parenthood; having a child with severe disabilities can be rewarding, but it is also difficult, and denying the difficulty is a disservice. The political left conflates access to abortion and abortion itself. In this view, the "responsible" choice is to prevent the suffering a disabled child will endure. But all children suffer, and we remain a procreative race. The putative suffering of disabled children can be a smoke screen. Would-be parents often imagine the suffering erroneously; they confuse how it feels to lose an ability (to be suddenly bereft of hearing) with how it feels to live healthily with a variant body (to be deaf all your life). Further, they confuse their own discomfort with their child's.

The Value of Choice

A lobby of the would-have-been-aborted militate against terminations; some have greeted the North Dakota laws as a humanitarian breakthrough. I can empathize with their concern, because I suspect my parents would have considered termination very seriously if they had somehow known I would be gay. I imagine a eugenic world in which medical advances could allow parents to abort fetuses destined to be like me in this regard, and the thought makes me sad. Still, choice is the hallmark and founding principle of democracy, and I would champion people's right to it. I would do so with a firm belief that choice strengthens families no matter what choice they make.

Both opponents and supporters of the right to selective termination tend to consider people who want to terminate—but choice is equally valuable to women who want to *continue* their pregnancies. Of the five thousand five hundred children born with Down syndrome in the United States each year, about six hundred and twenty-five are born to women who had a prenatal diagnosis. I have interviewed many such women, and, without exception, they were glad they had been able to think about the pregnancy and make a positive, affirming decision to keep it. Tierney Temple Fairchild, whose fetus had a prenatal Down syndrome diagnosis, wrote, in words I quote in my book, "I had a choice, and I chose life.

Does that make me pro-choice or pro-life? Our political parties tell us we can't have it both ways. . . . I chose life, but I am thankful I had the choice."

North Dakota's legislation [temporarily blocked by a court order in July 2013] attempts to interfere in the race between medical and social advancement. On the medical front, it's getting easier and easier to pick up genetic conditions earlier and earlier. At the same time, on the social front, people with genetic anomalies who were once hidden away in darkness and left to die young are writers, actors, activists. New strategies for early intervention have allowed people with Down syndrome to secure accomplishments that were once unimaginable; some are living independently; life expectancies have soared. People with forms of deafness that can be detected prenatally are members of a thriving deaf culture. People with achondroplastic dwarfism, also detectable prenatally, are more readily accepted than ever before, with more accommodations than ever before. We need only to bear collective witness to these changes. It will get harder to select against people in these categories not because of tyrannical laws, but because we see so much more joy in their lives.

Periodical and Internet Sources Bibliography

The following articles have been selected to supplement the diverse views presented in this chapter.

Daniel Allott	"The Fourth Trimester Abortion," *American Spectator*, March 21, 2012.
Centers for Disease Control and Prevention	"Global Initiative to Eliminate Folic Acid–Preventable Neural Tube Defects," November 14, 2011. www.cdc.gov.
Matthew Hennessey	"Down Syndrome and the Purpose of Prenatal Testing," *First Things*, August 1, 2011.
Ashley Herzog	"Abortion for Disabled Babies: Who's to Blame?," Townhall.com, February 14, 2013.
Nelson Jones	"Justifying Infanticide," *New Statesman*, March 1, 2012.
Jaime Staples King	"Not This Child: Constitutional Questions in Regulating Noninvasive Prenatal Genetic Diagnosis and Selective Abortion," *UCLA Law Review*, October 2012.
Joseph A. Komonchak	"Wrongful Birth, Wrongful Life?," *Commonweal*, March 10, 2012.
Warren C. Plauche	"Move to Prevent Birth Defects," *Atlanta Journal-Constitution*, June 16, 2012.
R.R. Reno	"Life Too Inconvenient for Life," *First Things*, June–July 2012.
William Saletan	"Fetal Flaw: The Abortion Politics and New Prenatal Tests," *Slate*, June 1, 2012. www.slate.com.
Fay Voshell	"Infanticide on Demand," *American Thinker*, March 1, 2012.

For Further Discussion

Chapter 1

1. On the basis of what you have read in the viewpoints in this chapter, what are two of the more serious birth defects and two of the less serious birth defects discussed?

2. Most of the birth defects discussed in this chapter can be diagnosed, with some level of certainty, prior to birth. What are two reasons that the diagnosis of a birth defect prior to birth could be beneficial?

Chapter 2

1. Christina Larson points to several studies that find a correlation between pollution and birth defects. Jacques Leslie discusses why it is difficult to prove that any particular pollutant causes birth defects. What is the difference between correlation and causation? Which is easier to prove? Why?

2. The authors in this chapter who discuss the risks of assisted reproduction agree that there is research correlating a higher risk of birth defects with such technologies. Ronald Bailey claims that the risk is too small to dissuade people from using the technologies. At what point, if ever, would the risks become so great that an argument could be made against the use of such assisted reproduction technologies? Explain your answer.

Chapter 3

1. Darshak Sanghavi advocates the use of routine ultrasounds for prenatal screening. Thinking about the kind of tests that Erin Biba describes, do you think Sanghavi would also endorse routine genetic tests? Why or why not?

2. Several authors in this chapter discuss the relationship between prenatal testing and abortion. Do you think more testing will lead to more abortions? Why or why not? Cite from the viewpoints in your answer.

Chapter 4

1. Andrew Ferguson argues that support of abortion does not logically lead to support for infanticide. How might someone argue that support for abortion does not necessarily entail support for infanticide?

2. Andrew Solomon claims that women are pressured on both sides of the abortion issue when it comes to prenatal diagnosis of birth defects. Do you think Solomon would find any author in this chapter to have committed either the conflation of the political right or the political left that he describes? Why or why not?

Organizations to Contact

The editors have compiled the following list of organizations concerned with the issues debated in this book. The descriptions are derived from materials provided by the organizations. All have publications or information available for interested readers. The list was compiled on the date of publication of the present volume; names, addresses, phone and fax numbers, and e-mail and Internet addresses may change. Be aware that many organizations take several weeks or longer to respond to inquiries, so allow as much time as possible.

**American Congress of Obstetricians
and Gynecologists (ACOG)**
409 Twelfth St. SW, Washington, DC   20024-2188
(800) 673-8444
e-mail: resources@acog.org
website: www.acog.org

The American Congress of Obstetricians and Gynecologists is an organization for obstetricians and gynecologists, and other providers of women's health care. ACOG aims to provide education worldwide, improve health care for women through practice and research, lead advocacy for women's health care issues nationally and internationally, and provide organizational support and services for members. Among its other publications, ACOG has several fact sheets on the topic of birth defects, including "Screening for Birth Defects."

American Medical Association (AMA)
515 N. State St., Chicago, IL   60654
(800) 621-8335
website: www.ama-assn.org

The American Medical Association is a professional association of physicians and medical students. It works to promote scientific advancement, improve public health, and invest in the doctor and patient relationship. The AMA provides information on its website about a variety of medical tests, including its recommendations regarding prenatal testing.

American Society of Human Genetics (ASHG)

9650 Rockville Pike, Bethesda, MD   20814-3998
(301) 634-7300 • fax: (301) 634-7079
website: www.ashg.org

The American Society of Human Genetics is the primary professional membership organization for human genetics specialists worldwide. It provides forums for advancing genetic research, enhancing genetics education, and promoting responsible scientific policies. ASHG publishes the *American Journal of Human Genetics* and an electronic newsletter, *SNP-IT*.

American Society of Law, Medicine, and Ethics (ASLME)

765 Commonwealth Ave., Ste. 1634, Boston, MA   02215
(617) 262-4990 • fax: (617) 437-7596
e-mail: info@aslme.org
website: www.aslme.org

The American Society of Law, Medicine, and Ethics is a nonprofit educational organization focused on the intersection of law, medicine, and ethics. The organization aims to provide a forum to exchange ideas in order to protect public health, reduce health disparities, promote quality of care, and facilitate dialogue on emerging science. ASMLE publishes two journals: the *Journal of Law, Medicine & Ethics* and the *American Journal of Law & Medicine*.

Birth Defect Research for Children, Inc. (BDRC)

976 Lake Baldwin Ln., Ste. 104, Orlando, FL   32814
(407) 895-0802
e-mail: staff@birthdefects.org
website: www.birthdefects.org

Birth Defect Research for Children, Inc. is a nonprofit organization that provides parents and expectant parents with information about birth defects and support services for their children. It sponsors the National Birth Defect Registry, a research project that studies associations between birth defects and exposures to radiation, medication, alcohol, smoking, chemicals, pesticides, lead, mercury, dioxin, and other environmental toxins. The BDRC publishes research on the causes of birth defects on its website.

Center for Bioethics & Human Dignity (CBHD)
Trinity International University, Deerfield, IL   60015
(847) 317-8180 • fax: (847) 317-8101
e-mail: info@cbhd.org
website: www.cbhd.org

The Center for Bioethics & Human Dignity (CBHD) aims to explore the nexus of biomedicine, biotechnology, and humanity. Within a Judeo-Christian and Hippocratic framework, CBHD engages in research, theological and conceptual analysis, charitable critique, and teaching. CBHD publishes the quarterly journal *Dignitas.*

Center for Genetics and Society (CGS)
1936 University Ave., Ste. 350, Berkeley, CA   94704
(510) 625-0819 • fax: (510) 665-8760
e-mail: info@geneticsandsociety.org
website: www.geneticsandsociety.org

The Center for Genetics and Society is a nonprofit information and public affairs organization working to encourage responsible uses and effective societal governance of the new human genetic and reproductive technologies. It works with scientists, health professionals, and civil society leaders to oppose applications of new human genetic and reproductive technologies that objectify and commodity human life and threaten to divide human society. CGS publishes fact sheets, reports, and the weblog *Biopolitical Times.*

Centers for Disease Control and Prevention (CDC)
1600 Clifton Rd., Atlanta, GA   30333
(800) CDC-INFO (232-4636)

e-mail: cdcinfo@cdc.gov
website: www.cdc.gov

The Centers for Disease Control and Prevention is one of the major operating components of the US Department of Health and Human Services. The CDC aims to create the expertise, information, and tools that people and communities need to protect their health, including work to identify causes of birth defects, find opportunities to prevent them, and improve the health of those living with birth defects. The CDC performs research into the causes of birth defects through its National Birth Defects Prevention Study (NBDPS) and sponsors state-based tracking systems to track the occurrence of birth defects.

Council for Responsible Genetics (CRG)
5 Upland Rd., Ste. 3, Cambridge, MA   02140
(617) 868-0870 • fax: (617) 491-5344
e-mail: crg@gene-watch.org
website: www.councilforresponsiblegenetics.org

The Council for Responsible Genetics is a nonprofit organization dedicated to fostering public debate about the social, ethical, and environmental implications of genetic technologies. It works through the media and concerned citizens to distribute accurate information and represent the public interest on emerging issues in biotechnology. The CRG publishes *GeneWatch*, a periodical dedicated to monitoring biotechnology's social, ethical, and environmental consequences.

Ethics and Public Policy Center (EPPC)
1730 M St. NW, Ste. 910, Washington, DC   20036
(202) 682-1200 • fax: (202) 408-0632
website: www.eppc.org

The Ethics and Public Policy Center is dedicated to applying the Judeo-Christian moral tradition to critical issues of public policy. Through its core programs, such as Bioethics and

American Democracy, the EPPC and its scholars work to influence policy makers and to transform the culture through the world of ideas. EPPC publishes *The New Atlantis*, a quarterly journal about technology with an emphasis on bioethics.

Genetics and Public Policy Center

Johns Hopkins University Berman Institute of Bioethics
Washington, DC   20036
(202) 663-5971 • fax: (202) 663-5992
e-mail: gppcnews@jhu.edu
website: www.dnapolicy.org

The Genetics and Public Policy Center works to help policy makers, the press, and the public understand the challenges and opportunities of genetic medicine. The center conducts legal research and policy analysis, performs policy-relevant social science research, and crafts policy recommendations. Available at the center's website are numerous reports and testimony transcripts, including the report "Tables of Direct-to-Consumer Genetic Testing Companies and Conditions Tested."

The Hastings Center

21 Malcolm Gordon Rd., Garrison, NY   10524-4125
(845) 424-4040 • fax: (845) 424-4545
e-mail: mail@thehastingscenter.org
website: www.thehastingscenter.org

The Hastings Center is a nonprofit bioethics research institute that works to address fundamental ethical issues in the areas of health, medicine, and the environment as these issues affect individuals, communities, and societies. The center conducts research and education and collaborates with policy makers to identify and analyze the ethical dimensions of policy making. The Hastings Center publishes two periodicals: the *Hastings Center Report* and *IRB: Ethics & Human Research*.

March of Dimes Foundation

1275 Mamaroneck Ave., White Plains, NY   10605
(914) 997-4488
website: www.marchofdimes.com

The March of Dimes Foundation works to help women have full-term pregnancies and healthy babies. It conducts research and offers information to families. The March of Dimes publishes the results of research and information on a variety of birth defects, available at its website.

National Human Genome Research Institute (NHGRI)
Communications and Public Liaison Branch
Bethesda, MD   20892-2152
(301) 402-0911 • fax: (301) 402-2218
website: www.genome.gov

A branch of the National Institutes of Health (NIH), the NHGRI led the NIH's contribution to the International Human Genome Project, which had as its primary goal the sequencing of the human genome. The NHGRI supports the development of resources and technology that will accelerate genome research and its application to human health. The NHGRI has many educational tools available on its website, including lectures and handouts from its Current Topics in Genome Analysis lecture series.

Bibliography of Books

Rachel Adams

Raising Henry: A Memoir of Motherhood, Disability, and Discovery. New Haven, CT: Yale University Press, 2013.

Michael Arribas-Ayllon, Srikant Sarangi, and Angus Clarke

Genetic Testing: Accounts of Autonomy, Responsibility, and Blame. New York: Routledge, 2011.

Mary Ann Baily and Thomas H. Murray, eds.

Ethics and Newborn Genetic Screening: New Technologies, New Challenges. Baltimore: Johns Hopkins University Press, 2009.

Amy Julia Becker

A Good and Perfect Gift: Faith, Expectations, and a Little Girl Named Penny. Bloomington, MN: Bethany House, 2011.

Jeffrey A. Brune and Daniel J. Wilson

Disability and Passing: Blurring the Lines of Identity. Philadelphia: Temple University Press, 2013.

Kate Davies

Rise of the US Environmental Health Movement. Lanham, MD: Rowman and Littlefield, 2013.

Dena S. Davis

Genetic Dilemmas: Reproductive Technology, Parental Choices, and Children's Futures. New York: Oxford University Press, 2010.

Lennard J. Davis, ed.

Disability Studies Reader, New York: Routledge, 2010.

Masha Gessen
Blood Matters: From Inherited Illness to Designer Babies, How the World and I Found Ourselves in the Future of the Gene. Orlando: Harcourt, 2008.

Philippe Grandjean
Only One Chance: How Environmental Pollution Impairs Brain Development—and How to Protect the Brains of the Next Generation. Oxford: Oxford University Press, 2013.

John Harris
Enhancing Evolution: The Ethical Case for Making Better People. Princeton, NJ: Princeton University Press, 2010.

Alison Kafer
Feminist, Queer, Crip. Bloomington: Indiana University Press, 2013.

Bengt Källén
Epidemiology of Human Congenital Malformations. New York: Springer, 2013.

Heather E. Keith and Kenneth D. Keith
Intellectual Disability: Ethics, Dehumanization, and a New Moral Community. West Sussex, UK: Wiley-Blackwell, 2013.

Thomas Lemke
Perspectives on Genetic Discrimination. New York: Routledge, 2013.

Catherine Mills
Futures of Reproduction: Bioethics and Biopolitics. New York: Springer, 2011.

Keith L. Moore, T.V.N. Persaud, and Mark G. Torchia
Before We Are Born: Essentials of Embryology and Birth Defects. Philadelphia: Saunders/Elsevier, 2013.

Ronald Munson — *Intervention and Reflection: Basic Issues in Bioethics.* Belmont, CA: Wadsworth, 2013.

Carol Ann Rinzler — *Leonardo's Foot: How 10 Toes, 52 Bones, and 66 Muscles Shaped the Human World.* New York: Bellevue Literary, 2013.

Nevin Hotun Sahin and Ilkay Gungor — *Birth Defects: Issues on Prevention and Promotion.* New York: Nova Science, 2010.

Frida Simonstein, ed. — *Reprogen-ethics and the Future of Gender.* New York: Springer, 2009.

Terry L. Smith — *Modern Genetic Science: New Technology, New Decisions.* New York: Rosen, 2009.

Rickie Solinger — *Reproductive Politics: What Everyone Needs to Know.* New York: Oxford University Press, 2013.

Stefan Timmermans and Mara Buchbinder — *Saving Babies? The Consequences of Newborn Genetic Screening.* Chicago: University of Chicago Press, 2013.

Laura Tropp — *A Womb with a View: America's Growing Public Interest in Pregnancy.* Santa Barbara, CA: Praeger, 2013.

Carlos Valverde, ed. — *Genetic Screening of Newborns: An Ethical Inquiry.* New York: Nova Science, 2010.

Index

A

Abortion. *See* Pregnancy termination; Sex-selective abortions

Abortion, after birth
argument for, 136–137
logic of argument, 140–141
moral concerns over, 135–141
overview, 136
slippery slope argument, 139
surprising conclusions on, 138–139
as thought experiment, 140

Adjusted odds ratio (AOR), 84

Air pollution, worldwide, *64*

Alatorre, Maura, 77–78

Alatorre, Miguel, 73

Alcohol use/exposure, 18, 50, 123

Allott, Daniel, 122

Alpha-fetoprotein (AFP) test, 46, 97

Alzheimer's disease, 37, 116

American Congress of Obstetricians and Gynecologists (ACOG), 96, 97, 108, 109, 146

Americans United for Life (AUL), 161

Americans with Disabilities Act (ADA)
discrimination clause, 154
overview, 128, 153
public attitudes over, 153–155
public biases and, 155–156
social norms and, 152–156

Amniocentesis test
costs and benefits of, 144–146
diagnosis with, 127

false negatives, 105
new recommendations for, 146–147
overview, 41, 90–91, 143
process of, 104, 120, 160
risk of, 97, 101–102, 125, 146–147
should be offered more, 142–147
as standard recommendation, 143–144
in wanted and viable pregnancies, *145*

Angel, Bradley, 72

Anophthalmia, 84

Antibiotic use and birth defects
advice for doctors, 85–87
case-controlled studies, 85
concerns over, 83–87
FDA drug risks, 86
overview, 84
specific antibiotics, 84–85

Archives of Pediatric and Adolescent Medicine (magazine), 84

Ariosa Diagnostics, 103, 111

Assisted reproductive technologies (ART), 79–82

Atlantic Monthly (magazine), 62

Atresia valve defect, 24, 26

Atrial septal defect (ASD), 22–23, 29, 84

Australia, 19, 137

Austria, 19

B

Baby Doe Amendment (1984), 15–16

179

D